Boys Who Rocked the World

HEROES FROM KING TUT TO BRUCE LEE

MICHELLE ROEHM McCANN

& THE EDITORS OF BEYOND WORDS PUBLISHING

ALADDIN
New York London Toronto Sydney New Delhi

BEYOND WORDS
Hillsboro, Oregon

ALADDIN
An imprint of Simon & Schuster
Children's Publishing Division
1230 Avenue of the Americas
New York, NY 10020

BEYOND WORDS
20827 N.W. Cornell Road, Suite 500
Hillsboro, Oregon 97124-9808
503-531-8700 / 503-531-8773 fax
www.beyondword.com

This Aladdin/Beyond Words edition October 2012

For information about special discounts for bulk purchases, please contact
Simon & Schuster Special Sales at 1-866-506-1949 or business@simonandschuster.com.

The Simon & Schuster Speakers Bureau can bring authors to your live event.
For more information or to book an event contact the Simon & Schuster Speakers Bureau at
1-866-248-3049 or visit our website at www.simonspeakers.com.

Managing editor: Lindsay S. Brown
Editors: Emmalisa Sparrow, Ali McCart, Michelle Roehm McCann, Laura O. Foster,
   Barbara Mann, Emily Strelow
Interior design: Sara E. Blum
Interior illustrations: David Hahn
The text of this book was set in Adobe Garamond Pro.
The illustrations for this book were rendered in Adobe Illustrator.

Manufactured in the United States of America 0912 FFG

10 9 8 7 6 5 4 3 2 1

Library of Congress Cataloging-in-Publication Data

Boys who rocked the world / [edited by] Michelle Roehm McCann and the editors of
   Beyond Words Publishing.
   p. cm.
   Includes bibliographical references.
   1. Boys—Biography—Juvenile literature.   2. Heroes—Biography—Juvenile literature.
   3. Men—Biography—Juvenile literature. I. McCann, Michelle Roehm, 1968– II. Beyond
   Words Publishing.
   CT107.B65   2012
   920.71—dc23

                                                                                    2011050719

ISBN 978-1-58270-331-2 (pbk)
ISBN 978-1-58270-362-6 (hc)
ISBN 978-1-4422-5456-9 (eBook)

For Ronan, I love watching
you follow your passions.
I hope you never stop.
—Michelle

CONTENTS

—⁓—

In the profiles in this book, passages of literary narrative based on factual events were imagined by the authors in an attempt to draw the reader into the life and perspective of the profiled boy.

King Tutankhamun

APPROXIMATELY 1347–1329 BC ☀ PHAROAH ☀ EGYPT

As my eyes grew accustomed to the light...
I was struck dumb with amazement.

—HOWARD CARTER, ARCHAEOLOGIST, REFERRING TO THE DISCOVERY OF KING TUT'S TOMB

Ten-year-old Tutankhamun nervously approached the great Karnak Temple. The last in a long line of rulers, young Tut was to be crowned pharaoh of Egypt. It was now his job to oversee the largest empire in the world, which stretched from Africa to Asia. *Will I be remembered as a great leader too?* he wondered as he walked past the great monuments and statues of the pharaohs who had ruled before him. The cheers from the crowd at the temple grew to a deafening roar as the boy entered. Would the boy pharaoh bring prosperity back to Egypt? He was their last hope.

Several priests poured sacred water from golden urns over Tut. Then they placed the magnificent three crowns of Egypt on his head. There was the tall, white crown of Lower Egypt, then the red crown of Upper

1

Egypt, and finally the *khepresh*, a blue crown representing Egypt's vast armies. Thousands of Egyptians looked on in hushed silence as the priests balanced the triple crown on Tut's small head.

Even though his reign was brief—only nine years—Tut's dream to be remembered came true. Though he ruled over three thousand years ago, he is now the most well-known of all the Egyptian pharaohs. As ruler, he helped return a crumbling empire to its former prosperity and stability. His tomb, filled with an immense wealth of gold and priceless artifacts—as well as a mysterious curse—has only helped solidify young Tut's legend.

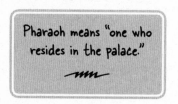

Pharaoh means "one who resides in the palace."

King Tut was born in 1347 BC in Egypt's rich, green Nile valley. His name, Tutankhamun, meant "strong bull," which suited Tut well. As a young man, he was praised for his strength and skills as a hunter of ostriches, peacocks, ibexes, gazelles, and wild hippos. His father was Pharaoh Akhenaten, who was not well-liked by Egyptians since he had defied the traditional religion, which had many gods, and singled out one god as worthy of worship. Akhenaten had also moved the capitol from Thebes to Amarna, further angering his people.

Growing up in Amarna, young Tut was a bit of a slacker. His older brother, Smenkare, was next in line to be pharaoh, so not much was expected of Tut. When he wasn't learning to read or write Egyptian hieroglyphs (pictures that represent words), Tut did what most kids do today: he goofed off. He hunted and raced around in chariots, played Senet, his favorite board game, and swam in the Nile with his siblings.

When Tut was seven years old, he received the shock of his life. Smenkare got very sick and died. Suddenly, Tut was destined to inherit all his father's duties as pharaoh of Egypt. No more slacking—it was time to cram! Tut's lessons got a lot harder as he prepared for his new role. Good thing he crammed. . . . Just two years later his father died. Only nine years old, Tut was now the ruler of the Egyptian empire and had the huge responsibility of unifying Egypt after his father's rocky reign.

Tut decided to bring back the traditional religion his father had outlawed and to return the capital to Thebes. When the young pharaoh moved back to the capital, a coronation ceremony was arranged so that all of Egypt could be introduced to their new boy king. Once crowned, Tut quickly ordered the rebuilding of the old temples that had fallen into disrepair during his father's reign. With the guidance of priests, he performed ceremonies to improve the harvest. (Most people in Egypt made their living from farming.) Tut was also in charge of Egypt's gigantic army, and with the help of his military advisers, he won several battles.

By age fifteen, Tut was growing into a strong and trustworthy leader.

> In his tomb, Tut was buried with over 140 pieces of jewelry, including 15 rings, 13 bracelets, many amulets, and a crown made of pure gold. He also had 93 pairs of shoes and 415 statues of servants to serve him in the afterlife.

He brought stability back to Lower and Upper Egypt, and comfort to people who honored the traditional religion. Tut was also proving to be a skilled negotiator, helping to solidify relations between Egypt's neighbors, Assyria and Babylonia. Egypt, which had experienced dark days during Akhenaten's reign, was making a comeback. Crops along the Nile were bountiful, and Egypt's many storehouses overflowed.

But King Tut's reign ended almost as quickly as it began. At the age of eighteen, King Tutankhamun suddenly died. No one is sure why. Was it disease? Was it an injury from one of his chariot rides? It's still a mystery today. Many scholars believe that Tut was assassinated by someone close to him who wanted his power. Maybe Tut was becoming too independent and would no longer listen to his advisers.

Whatever the cause of his death, it was a shock to the Egyptian people. The Egyptians believed that in order to preserve a person's *ka*, or soul, the dead body had to be mummified and placed in a tomb. Since Tut's death was unexpected, the Egyptians had to work frantically to put together a tomb for their king. Inside the tomb, they placed items that would keep their king entertained and comfortable in the afterlife. Then they created false chambers and hidden passageways to lead robbers away from its many treasures. Three thousand years passed, and shifting sands, grain by grain, covered the burial area—Tut's tomb vanished from sight.

Much of what we know today about King Tut's life comes from his tomb. In 1922 archaeologist Howard Carter uncovered a buried chamber in an area of Egypt called the Valley of the Kings, where most of the pharaohs were buried. Behind a secret door, Carter found the tomb of King Tut, almost perfectly preserved. It contained amazing artifacts—a golden mask and coffin, food vessels, jewelry, chariots, bows and arrows, statues of servants, game boards, furniture, and a magnificent throne.

Among the treasures, Carter discovered a clay tablet with hieroglyphs on it that warned: "Death shall slay with his wings whoever disturbs the peace of the pharaoh." He also found a statue that read: "It is I who drive back the robbers of the tomb with the flames of the desert. I am the protector of Tutankhamen's grave." With his eyes on the other treasures, Carter quickly forgot the warning words until two weeks later when Lord Carnarvon, the man who had paid for the expedition, got sick and died. Some thought it was from malaria, but others believed it was King Tut's curse. Next, a friend of Lord Carnarvon visited the tomb. The following day he got a high fever and suddenly died! Soon all sorts of deaths were linked to the discovery of Tut's tomb. Within ten years of opening the tomb, almost thirty people connected to the excavation had mysteriously died.

In ancient Egypt, men and women both wore black eye makeup made of lead ore. The makeup was considered stylish but also helped protect the Egyptians from eye infections and the harsh desert sun.

Finally, Dr. Ezzeddin Taha, who had examined several people involved in the excavation of Egyptian tombs, noticed that many of them suffered from a strange fungal infection. His research revealed that some fungi could survive for up to four thousand years in mummies and tombs! Symptoms of the infection were a high fever and an upper respiratory infection. Dr. Taha made a public statement saying that superstitions about King Tut's curse were silly, especially now that he had found the real reason people were dying. Coincidentally, after making this important scientific break-through, Dr. Taha died in a car crash. People today still debate whether Taha died because of the curse or because he had the fungal infection, which may have caused him to pass out and crash the car.

King Tut's death and tomb may be shrouded in mystery, but it is no mystery that, as one of the youngest pharaohs of Egypt, his memory lives on. His leadership and diplomacy skills helped strengthen Egypt's economy and return people's confidence in the pharaohs. His short life, his amazing tomb, and its curse have made him the most famous and well-known of all Egyptian kings. Like the ancient scribes of Egypt wrote, "Let your name go forth, while your mouth is silent." For no other pharaoh has this been more true than for King Tut.

> X-rays of the mummified Tut show that he might have died from a head injury—more proof for those who think he was murdered.

HOW WILL YOU ROCK THE WORLD?[1]

My plan is to get high up in the government and then propose the eco-car bill. There would be a recycling program where people would trade in their gas guzzling cars for a small amount of money. Charging stations for electric cars will be placed all around the country, and the electricity will be inexpensive. This bill would make it so a lot more people will use public transportation. This will affect many people because it will boost awareness about global warming and reduce our carbon footprint.

DUGAN MARIEB ☼ AGE 13

Galileo Galilei

1564–1642 ◎ INVENTOR AND PHYSICIST ◎ ITALY

Galileo, perhaps more than any other single person, was responsible for the birth of modern science.... Galileo was one of the first to argue that man could hope to understand how the world works, and, moreover, that we could do this by observing the real world.

—STEPHEN HAWKING, THEORETICAL PHYSICIST

Galileo was bored. After a week of studying math at the university, he had been looking forward to a good Sunday church service to fill his brain with more spiritual thoughts. Unfortunately, the visiting priest was so dull that Galileo couldn't keep his head from dropping onto his chest. Snapping it to attention, he overcompensated and threw his head back too far. Something on the ceiling caught his eye. A lamp, hanging from a chain high overhead, was swaying in the air currents. Its rhythmic arcs almost put him back to sleep, but then Galileo noticed something that surprised him: there seemed to be a pattern to the swings.

6

Wide awake now, he used his own pulse to time how long it took the lantern to swing from one end of its arc to the other. He realized something: each swing took the same amount of time, whether the lantern had swung wide in a new breeze, or had settled into a barely noticed sway when the air currents quieted.

Duh, you might say; that seems obvious. But it wasn't a *duh* then. People four hundred years ago had hardly a clue about what made the physical world work. With this observation, eighteen-year-old Galileo discovered the way to invent the first accurate mechanical clock, beginning a lifetime of experiments to figure out how the world works. He was the world's first physicist (a scientist who studies matter and energy and how they interact).

Galileo's curiosity would nearly get him killed later in life, but it also started humans down the road of knowledge to mechanics, electricity, radiation, and nuclear reactions. From a boring church service in Pisa in 1583 to a walk on the moon in 1969, and finally to nanotechnology today, there have been curious men and women, pulling more and more from the spool of scientific knowledge that Galileo started to unravel.

> Galileo said that a lock of wool and a piece of lead, if in a vacuum (with no air resistance), would fall at the same rate. In 1971, astronaut David Scott stood on the moon and dropped a feather and a hammer at the same time. They both fell side by side to the moon's surface. He remarked: "This proves that Mr. Galileo was correct."

Galileo's greatness came from his skepticism: he refused to believe something just because everyone else did. He came by this naturally; as a boy, Galileo had been taught by his father, who hated close-minded people, especially if they were in a position of authority.

By the time Galileo was eleven, his father could not keep up with his thirst for knowledge, so he sent his son to a monastery school. The peaceful life inside the monastery walls totally appealed to Galileo, so much so that, at thirteen, he volunteered to begin training as a monk. His dad was horrified and instantly nixed the idea: Galileo needed to pick a career that would generate enough money to help support the family. And four hundred years ago, just like today, doctors got paid big bucks. So, at his father's insistence, when Galileo was seventeen he entered the University of Pisa to study medicine. But he was not interested in medicine, and he argued with his father to be allowed to study math—a profession that would help him figure out how the world worked.

He must have been a good arguer because his father gave in. As Galileo later said of his passion for math:

> ... the universe cannot be understood unless one first learns to comprehend the language and interpret the characters in which it is written. It is written in the language of mathematics, and its characters are triangles, circles and other geometrical figures, without which it is humanly impossible to understand a single word of it ...[2]

At Pisa, Galileo kept on arguing with people who supposedly knew more. He argued so much that his teachers nicknamed him *Il Attaccabrighe*, "the Wrangler." What was he arguing about? Galileo felt that the facts they were teaching should not be accepted until someone had tested them.

When he was twenty-one, Galileo left school without earning a degree. Four years later, he was back, this time as an instructor. He began teaching math and went back to his old argumentative ways. At that time, universities were still following the teachings of Aristotle, who had lived 1,800 years earlier. One thing Aristotle had said was that the heavier an object was, the faster it would fall. Aristotle had never actually tried it; it just seemed to logically flow from other things he had observed.

Galileo easily proved this idea wrong: he climbed the Leaning Tower of Pisa and dropped two lead balls, one weighing much more than the other. As his critics watched, an 1,800-year-old "truth" was overturned:

both objects fell to the earth at exactly the same speed. By using public stages like this, Galileo became popular and changed many people's minds. But his popularity and ideas also created enemies, and he got fired from his job. Fortunately, friends got him a job at the University of Padua, near Venice. It had a reputation as being more open to new ideas, and Galileo was happy there. His fame grew as he invented and designed machines and instruments for various rulers and kings.

In 1609 the telescope was invented in Holland. It could magnify objects only up to three times, and it was merely used as a toy at parties. But Galileo saw other uses for the telescope and set out to improve it. By 1610 he had made a telescope so strong, it could be used in war to spy on approaching enemies. When he presented his telescope to the ruler of Venice, he was given a huge pay raise and a job for life. Orders poured in for his telescopes, and he became even more famous. He used his most powerful scopes—ones that could magnify an object thirty times—to look at the sky and discovered that the moon is full of mountains and craters. He also discovered another thing Aristotle was wrong about.

Aristotle had claimed that the Earth was the center of the universe —that the sun and all the other stars and planets revolved around the Earth. And the powerful Catholic Church agreed with him. If the Earth was the center of the universe, then that proved that the smartest creature on Earth, man, must be the center of the universe as well. Anyone who disagreed with this idea was considered an enemy of the church. And, at that time, the church was the same as the government. The punishment for disagreeing with it was torture or death.

Even though the Polish astronomer Nicolaus Copernicus had already said that the sun was the center of the universe, very few people believed him. Galileo did. His improved telescope allowed Galileo to prove that many of Copernicus's ideas were right. Galileo wrote a book, *The Starry Messenger*, arguing that the Earth was *not* the center of the universe. Instead, he said the Earth revolved around the sun. This book got him in big trouble. At age fifty-one, Galileo was forced to withdraw his ideas or risk death. To save his life, Galileo said that he had been wrong.

For the rest of his life, Galileo battled the church over his beliefs. Church officials often threatened him with prison, torture, and death in order to force him to lie about his discoveries, but he never totally gave in. He always continued writing and teaching the truth, even when the pope and the Inquisition (the Catholic Church's secret police) came after him. For the last eight years of his life, Galileo had to live under house arrest inside his home in Florence—but he never stopped conducting his experiments.

Some heroes would die rather than admit something that they don't believe in. Why didn't Galileo defend what he believed to the death? Maybe he wanted to live to make more discoveries. Or perhaps he knew that, whether he lived or died, the truth would eventually be known. And of course, it was. Today everyone, even the Catholic Church, believes that Galileo was right.

In the end, Galileo's greatest legacy is not any one of his inventions or discoveries, but his search for truth, even in the face of ignorant laws and rulers. In Galileo's day, the enemy of truth was people clinging to unproven beliefs. What is the enemy of truth today?

ROCK ON![3]

JACOB BARNETT

Jacob Barnett shocked his parents when, at three years old, he was solving five-thousand-piece puzzles and memorizing road maps. He taught himself geometry, trigonometry, algebra, and calculus, all within a week! He enrolled in his first college-level astrophysics class when he was eight, and at twelve, he was working on expanding Einstein's theory of relativity. Jacob has asperger's syndrome, a mild form of autism, but instead of being treated as though he were weird, his family, professors, and classmates show him respect and support as he explores concepts most people can't understand.

Blaise Pascal

1623–1662 ◈ MATHEMATICIAN, SCIENTIST, AND PHILOSOPHER
FRANCE

No matter how little time he had left for [math], he made such strides that at the age of sixteen he wrote a paper on the conic sections which was considered such an important intellectual achievement that it was said nothing so powerful had been seen since Archimedes.

—GILBERTE PASCAL, BLAISE'S SISTER

Twelve-year-old Blaise froze silently as he waited to hear the front door close, signaling his father's departure. With a thump, the wood door fell into place, and Blaise scurried to pull out his math notes. He'd been examining triangles and felt he was on the verge of discovering something important.

He loved shapes, but his father, Étienne, forbade him from learning mathematics, particularly geometry, until he was fifteen. Étienne believed that classic studies like Latin should be learned first and feared that his son would abandon them if he had the chance to study math. But Blaise couldn't help himself! The fact that his father had banished all books and objects related to math only fueled his desire to study them.

Blaise tapped his quill on the corners of the triangle he'd just drawn. He realized that if he combined the angles of all the corners, they would make two right angles, ninety degrees each. He quickly drew another triangle with all different angles. It was true again!

The young mathematician was so engrossed in his discovery that he didn't hear his father enter and walk up behind him until it was too late. He'd been found out.

"What are you doing?" his father asked.

"I'm . . ." Blaise fumbled for a good excuse but realized he had none. "I'm investigating a certain matter."

Étienne leaned over to examine his son's notes. Without a word, he nodded, turned, and walked away. Later that night, Blaise's father explained to him that he had discovered the truth of Euclid's thirty-second proposition—that the angles of any triangle add up to 180 degrees.

> Blaise loved shapes. His most famous research has to do with cones, cycloids (the curve created if you were to track the movement of a specific point on a ball as it rolled in a straight line), and triangles.
>
> —m—

"I want you to have this." He held out a leather-bound book.

Blaise ran his fingers over the smooth cover—it was *Euclid's Elements, Book I.* His father was granting him permission to study math!

Blaise Pascal was born in a small town in France, but when his mother died when he was just three years old, his father moved Blaise and his three sisters to Paris. Étienne didn't like the schools in Paris, though, so he decided to teach his children himself, which is when he made the wretched no-math rule. After Blaise's secret math studies had been found out, though, his father let him study math as much as he wanted—as long as he continued to learn Latin—and he could even go to the mathematical academy meetings with his dad!

Age sixteen was a big year for Blaise, and not because he got his driver's license like most teenagers do today. He developed his first theorem—a mathematical theory that can be proven—calling it the mystic hexagram. Then he wrote a book called *Essay on Conic Sections*. When his father was relocated to Rouen to be a tax collector that same year, Blaise started thinking of a device that would help with all the math involved in his father's job. It would be complicated, though, because French money was not in multiples of ten. Instead, there were twelve diniers in a sol and twenty sols in a livre. But by 1645, he had it! Blaise had invented a calculating machine, much like the digital calculators we use today. It was called a Pascaline.

When his father suffered a terrible accident and couldn't leave the house, the Pascals found support in the religious community, particularly the Jansenists. People from the church came to the house to help Blaise and his sisters and to teach them about a convent called Port Royal.

At this time, Blaise was still studying math and conducting experiments. He was fascinated with atmospheric pressure and the possibility of a vacuum—a place where no atmospheric pressure exists. In 1648 he proved that pressure in the atmosphere decreases the farther it is from the Earth. From this, he deduced that space must be a vacuum. René Descartes, another famous French mathematician at the time, often argued with Blaise about this theory, but we now know that Blaise was right.

Blaise also developed the theory of probability with Pierre de Fermat. The

Blaise studied a certain kind of triangle so much, it was named after him, even though he wasn't the first person to work with it.

```
              1
            1   1
          1   2   1
        1   3   3   1
      1   4   6   4   1
    1   5  10  10   5   1
```

Pascal's triangle is made up of numbers, the top row being a one. Moving down from there, numbers in rows are determined by adding the two numbers above them. It may sound simple, but the mathematical formula for this is:

$$\binom{n}{k} = \binom{n-1}{k} + \binom{n-1}{k-1}$$

two men realized they had been thinking the same thing at almost the same time and decided to work together. They focused on the dice problem, which asks how many times one must throw a pair of dice before double sixes can be expected, and the problem of points, which asks how to divide the stakes in an unfinished game of dice.

The more Blaise learned about Jansenism during this time, though, the more he focused on religion. Jansenism teaches that followers should devote all their time to God, so in 1654, three years after his father died, Blaise moved to Port Royal. From this time on, his mathematical writings are rare and short, though often profound. He did take on philosophical and religious writing, though, especially when his friend Antoine Arnauld went to trial for his Jansenist beliefs. Blaise anonymously published eighteen *Provincial Letters* that appeared to be between two friends—one in the city and one in the country—who make fun of the Jesuits, the most influential Christians of the time.

> Blaise invented the syringe. Imagine what life would be like today without that!
>
> —mm—

Blaise also wrote *Pensées*, his philosophy on religion. Here, his writing maintains his methodical writing style and sometimes sounds almost as if he's solving theorems of geometry or probability. He writes, "If God does not exist, one will lose nothing by believing in him, while if he does exist, one will lose everything by not believing."

Through much of his later life, Blaise suffered from stomach and head pain. Shortly after writing *Pensées*, the pain was so bad that Blaise could not fall asleep, and he lay awake thinking about math. He studied cycloids and decided he should challenge his fellow mathematicians, so he wrote two theorems, which he invited his colleagues to prove.

In his last years, he once again abandoned math and focused on the church, attending service after service whenever he wasn't giving to the poor.

HOW WILL YOU ROCK THE WORLD?

My dream is to become an aerospace engineer and create exploratory vehicles that go to Pluto and Proxima Centauri. I might design public shuttles to the moon and Mars with fuel tanks that could be fastened on in case of fire; sleeping cabins close to the galley, oxygen, and food supplies; and nuclear-powered engines. The ejectable sleeping cabins would have ram motors—motors that magnetically attract the hydrogen thinly spread through space and then burn it with an oxidizer. I can see it all now, me a famous aerospace engineer changing the way people travel.

NEIL FORRESTER ⚛ AGE 10

Kangxi

1654–1722 ◦ EMPEROR ◦ CHINA

*He deserves to be called a wise ruler through
the middle years of his reign.*

—FREDERICK W. MOTE, AUTHOR

Seven-year-old Xuanye looked on as his father moaned from his bed, sick with a fever and a rash. The Emperor Shunzhi had smallpox. Although Xuanye had survived the disease when he was younger, most people who developed the rash back then didn't live for long.

"It's up to you now," Shunzhi told his son. "Be a wise ruler."

Xuanye nodded solemnly. He would be the youngest emperor in the history of China.

Once Xuanye became emperor, his name was changed to Kangxi, and he was the second ruler in the Qing Dynasty of China. Because Kangxi was only seven when his father appointed him emperor, he also appointed four advisers to help him. These men were corrupt, though, and wanted the throne for themselves. They plotted to kick Kangxi out of his role as emperor, and one even had another one killed to beat out the competition! By the time Kangxi was fourteen, he'd had enough of it, and he fired the one remaining adviser so he could rule on his own.

Kangxi is known for bringing cultures together. He was multicultural —Manchurian on his father's side, Han Chinese on his mother's, and Mongolian on his grandmother's—and he felt he was a stronger person because of it. He learned the Mongolian tradition of riding horses, knew the Manchurian skill of hunting with a bow and arrow, and studied Confucian thought per the Han Chinese tradition.

Not everyone in Asia thought multiculturalism was a good thing, though, and Ming Dynasty followers in the south and in Taiwan resisted Kangxi's rule. Likewise, the northern borders were churning with unrest as Mongolians clashed against Kangxi and Russia invaded. Kangxi responded with many trips to the south to talk with the Ming followers. He showed his respect for their traditions and culture by asking them to write a history of the Ming Dynasty. Then he went to Mongolia. When the Mongolians saw Kangxi with his eighty thousand troops and hundreds of cannons, while they had just bows and arrows, they didn't fight back. Finally, Kangxi met with Russian rulers to sign a treaty about the border. It was the first time in a many years that China had not been at war.

Kangxi was also fascinated with Western culture. During his rule, Jesuit missionaries from the Christian world came to China. They taught Kangxi about astronomy and medicine, and he taught them about Confucian thought and Chinese traditions. This friendship came in handy when Kangxi caught malaria when he was forty. Chinese medicine didn't know how to cure the disease, so he

> Because the emperor's staff could not all be trusted, Kangxi developed a secure way of passing messages to his reliable officials who worked in other parts of the country. He'd put the message in a box, lock it, and then send it with the messenger. The official had the only other key for that box, so Kangxi knew no one else would read the message.

> Kangxi was the first Chinese emperor to play the piano. Pianos had been part of only Western culture before, but Kangxi thought they were beautiful.
>
> ～～

would have died for sure. But his missionary friends gave him quinine, which cured him. Unfortunately, the pope of the Christian church wasn't as open-minded as Kangxi, and he declared it unholy for anyone to practice Chinese traditions. Kangxi responded by asking the missionaries to leave China.

Kangxi loved language. When he was a boy, he memorized all the important Chinese texts, and as a father, he made his sons study them too. As a ruler, he'd already asked the Ming followers to compile a history of the dynasty, but he wanted people to be working on other books as well. He hired a committee to write a Chinese dictionary. In Chinese, words are represented by symbols—called characters—instead of combinations of letters. The dictionary the committee created for Kangxi include forty-seven thousand characters! Only about a fourth of those are used today, but that dictionary was used for about two hundred years. Kangxi also focused on literature. He hired another committee to compile the *Quantangshi*, an anthology of more than fifty thousand poems by 2,200 authors. New editions of this book are still being published today.

HOW WILL YOU ROCK THE WORLD?

I want to be a photographer for a nature magazine. I would like to take really interesting pictures of misunderstood or feared species and write articles about why we should respect them like any other animal. My role in this would be to provide the knowledge it takes to convince people to stop fearing strange animals and to start to know just how beautiful they truly are. Whether they're winged or clawed, scaled or finned, they are all wonderful, fascinating forms of life and need to be recognized as their true selves, not as monsters or nightmares, but as fellow creatures that can amaze us if we just take the time to discover them.

CAMERON LIVERMORE · AGE 12

Wolfgang Amadeus Mozart

1756–1791 ◦ COMPOSER ◦ AUSTRIA

*I declare to you on my honour that he is
the greatest composer who ever lived.*

—JOSEPH HAYDN, COMPOSER, SPEAKING OF MOZART

Five-year-old Wolfgang could not hold it in anymore. All morning the music had run through his head, and he just had to write it down. He waited impatiently until his father, Leopold, went out for a coffee with a friend. Grabbing a quill and his father's inkwell and forgetting that he had not yet learned to write, he filled a page with smudgy notes.

"What are you *doing*?!" Leopold burst in on the boy.

"I am writing a concerto. It will be done soon," replied Wolfgang calmly, already sure of himself. Both men laughed and winked at each other. How cute, they thought . . . the boy imitating his father, the court composer for the archbishop of Salzburg, Austria. But when Leopold read the notes, he began to cry for joy. His tiny son had indeed written a complicated and well-organized concerto.

This ink-stained beginning was the first of over six hundred pieces of music that Mozart wrote, many of them complex symphonies he created in one sitting. He said that, before he wrote a single note, he heard the entire piece in his head, sometimes with as many as twelve different instruments. He wrote feverishly, perfectly, with no revising. Many people then and now consider Mozart to be the greatest composer the world has ever known.

> Mozart's whole name was Johann Chrysostomus Wolfgang Gottlieb Mozart. Gottlieb means, in German, "God-loved." After dropping the first two names, and changing Gottlieb to its Latin synonym (AMA=love; DEUS=God), he was known as Wolfgang Amadeus Mozart.

Unlike today, when geniuses like Mark Zuckerberg earn big money from investors, in Mozart's day talented people could only find success if they won the favor of royalty. Instead of being seen as artists, they were seen merely as craftsman, like a good carpenter or tailor. If you had talent then, your only hope was to be noticed and rewarded by your king or queen.

Mozart's dad, knowing that he had a child prodigy on his hands, saw young Wolfgang as the family's ticket to fame and fortune. So when Wolfgang was six, his father took him and his sister Nannerl, who was also talented, on a three-year tour of Europe. Dressed up as a miniature adult, complete with a powdered white wig, Wolfgang performed musical tricks, like instantly playing any new piece given to him or playing the harpsichord with the keys hidden under a cloth.

Wolfgang and Nannerl played for the kings and queens of Austria, France, and England, and everyone loved the talented children. Love, however, did not pay the bills, and Wolfgang's father

> Beethoven was one of Mozart's piano students.

Young Mozart charmed the empress of Austria when he asked her little daughter, Marie, to marry him. Marie grew up to be the famous Marie Antoinette, queen of France. Perhaps she should've married Mozart—she died at the guillotine when rebels overthrew the French monarchy.

—◀◀◀—

was constantly frustrated by the stinginess of the royal families. They often would reward his children with nothing more than a golden snuffbox or some other small trinket.

When the family returned to Salzburg, the archbishop there accused Mozart's father of writing all the music his young son had composed. The archbishop locked Wolfgang in a palace room for a week and ordered him to write some music for the church. It took Wolfgang less than seven days to produce a musical score of 208 sheets of paper. The archbishop was convinced. When Mozart was just fourteen, he wrote and directed his first opera.

Wolfgang spent his entire childhood touring, except for brief visits back to Salzburg and time recovering from smallpox, typhoid, and other illnesses. These illnesses probably contributed to his early death. By age twenty-one, Wolfgang had traveled all over Europe, composing and performing sonatas, concertos, symphonies, church music, music for string quartets, and opera for kings and queens.

It is easy to think that geniuses have it easy. But with music flowing out of his fingertips as fast as most people form a sentence, Mozart had to answer to people who saw him as a freak of nature, a person who didn't have to work hard:

If you want to learn more about Mozart's life, check out the movie AMADEUS.

—◀◀◀—

It is a mistake to think that the practice of my art has become easy to me. I assure you, dear friend, no one has given so much care to the study of composition as I. There is scarcely a famous master in music whose works I have not frequently and diligently studied.[4]

Despite his genius and amazing devotion to his craft, as an adult, Mozart usually could not scrape together enough coins to pay for food, fuel, or rent. He was often at the mercy of stingy noblemen who took advantage of his skills while paying him very little to write what he considered boring, uninspired pieces for their parties. When he did finally find a patron, he couldn't even ask for a decent salary, but instead had to humbly take whatever was offered. He also had to suffer the embarrassment, even though he was praised as the most divinely inspired composer ever, of being seated at the servants' table.

> Once a friend stopped by Mozart's apartment and found him and his wife waltzing wildly. "What are you doing dancing with no music?" he asked. "Keeping warm," answered Mozart. The couple had no money for firewood.

Even though the times he lived in made it hard to earn money, Mozart compounded his own problems: when he did have money, he blew it. Have you ever noticed that the smartest kid in class can never find his calculator, or that your brilliant mother is always losing her purse? Sometimes the smartest people seem to have gaping brain-holes for the more practical matters of life. That was Mozart. Because he was so bad at making and keeping money, Mozart never earned enough to relax. Instead of being able to compose music, which was all he wanted to do, Mozart had to teach piano most of the day, perform at small parties in the evenings, and then squeeze in his composing during the very latest hours.

Mozart worked nonstop and grew weaker and more exhausted as he got older. At thirty-five he received a fearful omen: a mysterious stranger appeared at his door and asked him to write a requiem mass (a funeral song). The stranger would not reveal his identity, and as Mozart worked on the requiem, his health got worse and worse. He became convinced the stranger was a messenger from God and that he was writing his own funeral music. He was. Mozart died before the piece was finished.

Mozart was famous in his lifetime and even more famous today. There has never been another genius like him. The music that poured out of Mozart more than two hundred years ago is still played, in television commercials, in movie soundtracks, and of course in concert halls. You may not know that you know Mozart, but you do; his music is all around us.

ROCK ON!

NOAH GRAY-CABEY

Most known for his acting roles in *Heroes* and *My Wife and Kids*, Noah Gray-Cabey actually got his start as a pianist. He started playing when he was just a toddler, and when he was five, he set the record as the youngest person to ever play at the Sydney Opera Hall. It was actually his musical talent that caught the eye of television shows like *The Tonight Show with Jay Leno* and *Dateline*, which then led to appearances and finally recurring roles on hit series. Noah also cofounded Action in Music, which helps spread music around the world.

John Quincy Adams

1767–1848 ◈ PRESIDENT, POLITICIAN, AND ABOLITIONIST
UNITED STATES

*If your actions inspire others to dream more, learn more, do more,
and become more, you are a leader.*

—JOHN QUINCY ADAMS

Seven-year-old John Quincy ducked his head behind a rock as he heard a cannon fire in the distance. His mother, Abigail Adams, sat by his side atop Penn's Hill as they watched the battle unfold in the Massachusetts valley below them.

"Why are they fighting, Mother?" John asked as he watched men approach Charlestown, Massachusetts, with blazing torches.

"England wants us to be part of their country," Abigail explained. "But we don't want to be anymore, so we have to fight for our freedom."

John nodded solemnly as he remembered his father, politician John Adams, having discussions with other men in their parlor about the things England was trying to force them to do, like pay higher taxes.

His father had been working in Europe as a diplomat trying to reach a peaceful resolution, but it looked like England didn't want to be peaceful.

The Battle of Bunker Hill lasted only about three hours, but it would be years before America and England stopped fighting. That day on Penn's Hill, John Quincy Adams vowed to himself that he would help shape this country that the soldiers in front of him were fighting for.

John Quincy was born on July 11, 1767, and was truly the child of revolutionaries. During his early life, he traveled with his father to Europe on his diplomatic trips. He later watched as his father negotiated and signed the Treaty of Paris, which recognized the United States of America as independent from England, and he applauded when his father became the country's first vice president and then the second president. His mother supported her husband intellectually, often discussing politics with him and advising him in his role as diplomat. She later encouraged John Quincy to pursue politics as well.

> John Quincy Adams's nicknames were Old Man Eloquent, for the long, flowing speeches he gave as president, and The Abolitionist, for his work against slavery during his later years.

By the time he was twenty-three, John had finished his studies at Harvard and was a practicing lawyer. He had also worked as a translator for US ministers, so when he was appointed to be minister to the Netherlands and later the Berlin Legation, he was excited. His mother urged him to take his experience one step farther, though, and to become even more active in politics. She wrote in a letter:

These are the times in which a genius would wish to live. It is not in the still calm of life, or the repose of a pacific station, that great characters are formed. . . . Great necessities call out great virtues. When a mind is raised, and animated by scenes that engage the heart, then those qualities which would otherwise lie dormant, wake into life and form the character of the hero and the statesman.

John Quincy Adams remembered his boyhood vow on Penn's Hill, and he accepted an appointment to the Massachusetts State Senate in 1802 and then to the US Senate in 1803.

On the Senate floor, John began to assert his belief in the importance of the common good. He voted for the Louisiana Purchase, which expanded America all the way to the Rocky Mountains, and he also supported President Monroe's Embargo Act of 1807. This was a controversial topic because the embargo would shut down all of America's imports and exports, which were the main methods of making money in New England and other parts of the United States. But whenever America sent off export ships to Europe, they were attacked in the Atlantic by British and French ships. Whenever America bought imports from England or France, they were just supporting the countries that were being hostile. Like President Monroe, John thought the embargo was the best way to protect America's ships without turning to violence. Despite opposition, the embargo was passed. John had stood up for what he believed was right.

> By the time John became president, Europe already had 130 public observatories. America didn't have any yet!

John also worked as the secretary of state for President Monroe. In this role, he healed America's relationship with England so they could be peaceful and support each other, and he also developed friendly relationships with other countries that would later help America. With John's help, the United States was growing and maturing.

When Monroe's second presidential term was coming to an end in 1825, John decided to run for president. After all, his father had been president, he'd enjoyed working for Monroe, and he had a grand vision for America's potential. The presidential race was close, though. There were four candidates: Andrew Jackson, John Quincy Adams, William H. Crawford, and Henry Clay, and none of them had a majority (51 percent or more) of votes. The House of Representatives turned to Clay, the person with the fewest votes, and asked him to show his support for one of the other three candidates. He liked John's presidential goals the best, so he voted for him. This made Jackson angry, and then when John appointed Clay as his secretary of state, the public accused John of bribing Clay to vote for him. It was not a good way to start his presidency.

But President John Quincy Adams was still dedicated to his grand plan to make America a better place. He focused on the common good of the nation, and he hoped to institute a national university and a national naval academy that would help develop the future leaders of the country. He also wanted to support science by improving the patent system so inventors could protect their ideas and make money off of them, and by building an astronomical observatory.

Other politicians and many of the people thought that John's goals weren't realistic, though. They argued that he was overambitious and that he only wanted to support the elite people while he ignored the people who worked on farms, in factories, and at other lower-class jobs. Because the president must have the support of Congress to do many things, most of John's presidential goals remained unfulfilled. When John's greatest role model—his father—died in 1826, he was devastated. Then tragedy struck again just after John's presidential term ended in 1829; his oldest son passed away. John retreated to his estate in Massachusetts, far away from the constant disputes in Washington, to garden and read in solitude.

Two years later, John was ready to work for his country again, and he was invited to join the House of Representatives. Even though some people thought it would be degrading for a former president to take a lesser office as a representative, John responded that one should never be ashamed of serving one's country and its people.

John Quincy Adams helped award the first-ever grant to the Smithsonian Institute, which was America's first foundation for scientific research.

Some historians believe the highlight of John Quincy Adams's career came during this time in the House of Representatives. He ardently fought against slavery, and in 1839 he proposed a constitutional amendment that would grant freedom to every child born of slave parents after July 4, 1842. But congressmen from the South who wanted to keep slavery issued a gag rule, meaning that Congress was not allowed to discuss slavery or abolitionism. This only made John want to talk about it even more! He argued that the gag rule went against the First Amendment's guarantee of freedom of speech, and he brought it up every time the House met until they finally withdrew the gag rule in 1844.

Another one of John's biggest accomplishments came during this time, but in the courtroom. In 1839 a ship named *Amistad* was on its way to America with a load of African people to be sold as slaves. The would-be slaves revolted, took over the ship, and brought it to New York, where slavery was illegal. The president at the time thought the Africans should be returned to the slave merchants, but John defended them as freemen in the Supreme Court. In November 1841, the thirty-five surviving Africans boarded another ship that would return them to their homeland.

As the years passed, John Quincy Adams was so respected by his fellow congressmen that they stood and applauded when he returned after a long absence due to a stroke. When he was eighty-one years old, John was speaking out against the US-Mexican War during a House meeting when he had a second stroke. He died two days later in the Capitol building. He is still considered one of America's most influential presidents.

> John finally fulfilled his dream of an American observatory. When he was 77 years old, he laid the cornerstone for an observatory being built in Cincinnati, Ohio.

HOW WILL YOU ROCK THE WORLD?

I will try to make the world better by making life easier for unprivileged children and the homeless. I want to contribute to fund-raisers that make their lives easier by building shelters and giving them beds and food. That is how I will contribute not only to society but also to the world.

JESUS GONZALEZ ☼ AGE 16

29

Louis Braille

1809–1852 ❉ TEACHER AND INVENTOR ❉ FRANCE

The blind can now work, they can study, they can sing, they can add their share to the good and happiness in the world. And it was Louis Braille . . . who found the golden key to unlock their prison door.

—HELEN KELLER, ADVOCATE FOR THE BLIND AND DEAF

The instructor tapped on his desk, calling the reading class to order. But this was no ordinary reading class. The embossed books used by the French Royal Institute for Blind Youth in 1819 were so special that the school owned just fourteen of them. This was ten-year-old Louis's first day in class, and he was thrilled: he would finally be able to read on his own!

Embossed books for the blind had been invented thirty years earlier. To make them, large letters were pressed into thick sheets of waxed paper, leaving impressions. Then, when the page was turned over, a blind person could read the letters by tracing their outlines with a finger. The only problem was, each page could hold just a few sentences, so the books were big and fat. You couldn't even hold one; it had to be propped up on an easel.

Still . . . it was reading, and after the seven years of darkness since he'd lost his sight, Louis was excited. But his excitement soon turned to disappointment. Louis found that tracing each letter with his finger took so long that by the time he got to the end of a sentence, he couldn't remember what it said at the beginning. Even if he could remember what he was reading, what good did it do? In all of France, there were just a handful of embossed books. They were too expensive to print and too big to store.

There must be a better way, Louis thought. For years the problem occupied his mind, and it ultimately evolved into the greatest gift to blind people that has ever been invented: braille, a reading system named for the boy who invented it. Without braille, the blind would never know the joys of losing themselves in a good novel or even reading sports scores—the daily tasks that sighted people take for granted.

Louis Braille lost his sight at age three, when he accidentally poked his eye with a tool in his father's harness-making shop in Coupvray, a small village twenty-five miles from Paris. The eye became infected, and when little Louis rubbed it, he accidentally spread the infection to the other eye as well. Within weeks of the accident, he was totally blind in both eyes.

His father made him a cane that allowed him to explore his physical surroundings, but the cane could only take him so far into the world. His blindness left him isolated: he couldn't play games, run through the woods, or climb trees with the other children.

Today Louis Braille rests in the Pantheon in Paris, the burial place of France's greatest heroes.

When Louis first experimented with sonography, he eagerly discussed his ideas with Captain Barbier. Barbier was not pleased to have his design questioned—especially by a kid! He insisted that it could not be changed. Good thing Louis didn't listen to him!

And two hundred years ago, the blind were thought to be mentally handicapped. People figured that if a person couldn't see, he or she couldn't think either. Blind people weren't welcome in schools or taught any trade or skill. If you were blind in Europe back then, you'd probably end up a beggar on the streets.

> eBraille is now being developed. It's a web-based system to transcribe and deliver any web page or computer file into braille to users anywhere.

Luckily, the village priest in Coupvray saw Louis for what he was: a normal boy who happened to be blind. Father Jacques Palluy taught Louis and convinced the schoolmaster to accept him as a pupil. As if to make up for his lack of vision, Louis's memory was phenomenal, and he learned rapidly—so rapidly that Father Jacques was able to get him into the Royal Institute for Blind Youth in Paris.

At the school Louis read his first books and acquired skills that would allow him to support himself. When he was thirteen, the institute had an important visitor, a man who would change Louis's life. Charles Barbier was a retired captain in the French army who had invented a military code based on dots and dashes punched with a stylus (a sharply pointed, pen-like tool) into strips of cardboard. The code allowed field commanders to silently give orders like "Advance" or "Withdraw" at night. When it occurred to Barbier that blind people might find it useful, he expanded his code so each word was broken into sounds and each sound was a different combination of dots and dashes. He called it sonography, or sound-writing.

Sonography looked complicated, but the school's director agreed to try it with the students. Louis became a sonography expert, but the more he learned about it, the more problems he found: since the symbols represented sounds, there was no way to show spelling, punctuation, or numbers. And many of the symbols were too big to read with the single touch of a finger. Sonography was so hard to use, many blind students gave up.

Louis didn't give up but began experimenting with sonography. From age thirteen to fifteen, his days were filled with classes and friends, but at night and on weekends he created patterns of dots, trying to find an easier system. Some nights, Louis lost track of time; as he sat on his bed punching dots, the rumbling of wagons outside told him that morning had come. His passion took a toll on his health, and he developed tuberculosis.

Then one night, as his classmates snored away, a brainwave hit Louis: the *sounds* were the problem. He had been stuck trying to work within Barbier's system when it was the system itself that was wrong. Instead of representing sounds, Louis created symbols that stood for the *letters* of the alphabet. Just like the alphabet sighted people use. His code was made up of six dots, like this:

1 ● ● 4

2 ● ● 5

3 ● ● 6

This code unit, called the braille cell, has space for six dots: two across and three down. For each letter of the alphabet, mark of punctuation, symbol, and number, Louis worked out a different arrangement of dots. Here's how his first name looks in braille:

L O U I S

Every letter and symbol could fit within the space of a fingertip. When he demonstrated his invention for the school's director, Dr. Pignier, he asked him to read aloud a paragraph from any book: "Read slowly and distinctly, as if you were reading to a sighted friend who was writing down your words." As Pignier read, Louis punched holes with his stylus onto a sheet of paper. It was so easy to do that he told Dr. Pignier, "You can read faster." Pignier finished reading and Louis finished "writing" at almost the same time. Then, as the amazed director watched, Louis turned the paper over and read, with his fingertips, the raised bumps his stylus had left—every word Dr. Pignier had dictated. The man was overwhelmed with emotion. He knew what this meant: a fifteen-year-old boy had just switched on the light of learning for blind people forevermore.

During the next few years, Louis improved and added to his system. At twenty, his system perfected, he wrote a book explaining it, called *Methods of Writing Words, Music, and Plain Song by Means of Dots, for Use by the Blind and Arranged by Them.* The braille system solved the main problems of the earlier embossed books. Since braille letters could fit under a person's fingertip, it was possible to read much faster. Braille letters took up about the same space as printed letters, so the books weren't so huge and expensive to produce. And best of all, because braille was like the regular alphabet that sighted people used, it was easy to learn.

At the school for the blind, Louis also learned to play musical instruments. He was so good that for the rest of his life he earned a living playing music in Paris churches.

Despite Dr. Pignier's enthusiasm, government officials were slow to change. They didn't want to give up their old embossed letter system and asked, "Why should blind people learn a different alphabet than the rest of us?" Obviously, they never had to read their embossed books! When Louis's school got a new director, even he refused to use braille. But so many students were smuggling styluses into the school and teaching one another braille, the new director had to give in.

Louis stayed at the institute his entire life, teaching and playing music. When tuberculosis overtook him at forty-three, his last words were, "I am convinced that my mission on earth is finished."

Imagine a life without reading: no internet, no computer games, no Harry Potter. Thanks to the invention of a teenage boy, millions of blind people only have to *imagine* that kind of a life.... They don't have to *live* it. Thanks to Louis, they can open a book, anytime, and read whatever they want. The horrible accident that blinded Louis Braille also gave him the will to create one of mankind's most humanitarian inventions.

ROCK ON!

TYRELL RHODES

When sixteen-year-old Tyrell Rhodes won an essay-writing contest, he was elated, but not just because it meant he was a good writer—the prize was a tour of the pilot training facility at Southwest Airlines. It wasn't totally new information for him (his mom worked in the Air Force), but it fueled his desire to become a pilot so much that he began taking pilot courses at Southwestern Illinois College. That's pretty amazing, especially for a boy with cerebral palsy, who was told he'd never be able to do things other kids could!

Los Niños Héroes

1828–1847 ◦ SOLDIERS ◦ MEXICO

Brave men don't belong to any one country.
I respect bravery wherever I see it.

—HARRY S. TRUMAN, US PRESIDENT, WHEN HE VISITED THE LOS NIÑOS HÉROES MONUMENT

Thirteen-year-old Francisco Márquez planted his feet on the ground and steadied his musket on the castle wall. Below, American soldiers were surrounding Chapultepec Castle—Mexico City's last hope to fight off the invaders and to keep its northern territory. Francisco looked down the barrel of his gun and sighted in on an enemy the way his teacher had taught him to. He'd never shot a gun this big before, but he was determined to defend his country in every way he could.

Nearby, army troops, town volunteers, and his friends were fighting too. Chapultepec Castle was normally a military academy where Mexican boys were trained to fight in the army. When Francisco had joined, he never would have guessed he would be fighting when he was still a boy!

The fighting between Mexico and the United States had started two years earlier, in 1845. Mexico was newly independent from Spain, and Americans wanted to settle in Texas. Mexico viewed this as a violation of its territory and fought back, but because American soldiers had better weapons and training, Mexico lost Texas.

The Mexican territory still extended north to the west of Texas, though—but not for long. American President James K. Polk was a firm believer in Manifest Destiny (the idea that God wanted America to stretch from "sea to shining sea"), and he sent the American military in to fight Mexico for the rest of its northern territory.

After nine battles, the Americans had advanced all the way to Mexico's capital—the last city to be captured before the United States would declare victory. Francisco reloaded his musket and aimed again. If he and his friends could help keep that from happening, they would, even if they had to die for their country.

Suddenly Francisco heard a loud yell, but he couldn't make out what General Nicolás Bravo had said. All around him, soldiers started lowering their guns. "He wants us to retreat," said Francisco's friend Juan de la Barrera, the oldest of the group at nineteen. The two looked around to their remaining four friends: Juan Escutia, Agustín Melgar, Fernando Montes de Oca, and Vicente Suárez. Agustín shook his head just slightly, but they all knew what he meant— they would keep fighting.

> The territory that America and Mexico were fighting for made up what is now Arizona, California, and Nevada as well as part of New Mexico and Colorado.

Though Mexico lost the Battle of Chapultepec and the Mexican–American War, those six boys went down in Mexican history as Los Niños Héroes, "the boy heroes." They fought for what they believed in, and they died for their country on that day in 1847.

One version of the legend says that the boys hung the Mexican flag back up every time it was shot down. Another relates that Juan Escutia feared for the safety of the flag as American troops closed in behind him, so he wrapped himself in the flag and jumped over the castle wall. Still another says that when the boys were the last six Mexican soldiers standing, they wrapped themselves in the flag, yelled, "*Viva Mexico!*" (Long live Mexico!), and jumped together to their death over the castle wall. And one claims that while Juan jumped over the castle wall, the other five boys killed themselves with their daggers so they wouldn't be taken prisoner. One thing is for certain, though—the boys died heroically.

Today, streets, schools, and parks all over the country are named after Los Niños Héroes. There's even a band that bears their name, and the entrance of Chapultepec Park is adorned with a statue commemorating the six boy heroes. In the spring of 1947, almost one hundred years after the Battle of Chapultepec, US President Harry Truman visited the monument and laid a wreath at its base. Newspapers report that the Mexican people felt a hundred-year-old wound heal that day.

HOW WILL YOU ROCK THE WORLD?

When I grow up I will invent a way to turn missiles around and shoot them back to where they were launched. If there is another world war, the people in America will be safe from nuclear or other missile bombardment. I will also invent a new kind of antiaircraft flack ammo. It will be tiny computer chips that download a virus if they come in contact with any wire, so that you can take over an airplane remotely.

NOAH SCHWARTZ · AGE 13

CRazy HoRse

APPROXIMATELY 1841–1877 ◉ WARRIOR AND LEADER
NORTH AMERICA

One does not sell the earth upon which the people walk.

—CRAZY HORSE

Curly was shocked. He had just seen US troops shoot Chief Conquering Bear in the back while he was negotiating with them for peace. These white men cared little for the Sioux or their way of life. They slaughtered buffalo for sport, introduced new diseases that the Sioux had no protection against, and sold them whiskey, which made them sick. Curly hoped that a vision from the Great Spirit, *Wakan Tanka*, would show him how to help and protect his people.

For three days, thirteen-year-old Curly lay down in an isolated spot on the prairie—no food, no shelter—praying for a vision. To keep awake, he lay on sharp stones. By the third day without sleep, Curly was exhausted. He was weak from hunger, and his body was sore from the rocks. And still, *Wakan Tanka* had not given him a vision.

The Sioux believed buffalo were sacred animals, and when they killed one, they used every part of it—the bladders became water bags, bones became tools and knives, and hides became blankets, clothing, drums, and tepees. White settlers, on the other hand, paid $10 to ride a buffalo hunting train. In one day on the train, a single person with a gun could shoot more than 100 buffalo— which they just left to rot! In 20 years, more than 30 million buffalo were massacred. By the 1900s, the great buffalo herds were gone.

Pulling his aching body up off the ground, Curly searched for his pony. Suddenly, the air grew hazy. A great warrior appeared, riding a pinto similar to Curly's own horse. Most Sioux warriors carried scalps as war trophies, but this warrior had none and wore only a single feather in his hair. Behind the mysterious rider, storm clouds gathered. Gunfire and arrows rained from the sky, and a lightning bolt shot down, grazing the warrior's face. Then, as quickly as he had appeared, the strange warrior melted away. Though Curly didn't realize it then, this vision would change his life forever. Curly would one day become the rider in his dream—a fearless warrior and champion for the Sioux. People far and wide would know him as Crazy Horse.

Born in about 1841 in South Dakota's Black Hills, Crazy Horse was first named Curly because of his wavy, light-brown hair. Curly's mother died when he was a baby, and his father was a holy man. As a young child, his Sioux tribe rarely stayed in one place for more than a few days because they followed the buffalo herds. Sioux riders were outstanding horsemen. They were so skilled on their pintos that they could fight, hunt, and even sleep on horseback!

By the time he was fifteen, Curly was a great horseman and hunter, but his true destiny was still unclear. To gain insight into Curly's future, Curly and his father built a sweat lodge. Sioux sweat lodges were usually small tents built around a pit containing hot rocks and were used to gain self-awareness, purification, and higher knowledge.

Curly, who had never told anyone about his vision, finally revealed to his father what he had seen two years earlier. His father told him that one day he would be a great warrior—the dream rider in his vision. After several years of training, seventeen-year-old Curly was ready to go to battle. To protect him, Curly's father made a special medicine powder of dried aster flowers and eagle's brain, which Curly was to put in his mouth and rub on his skin. Curly also wore a red-backed hawk feather and painted a lightning bolt down his nose to represent the warrior in his vision.

Curly's first battle was between the Sioux and the Arapaho tribes over land rights. After several hours of fighting, the Sioux were losing ground. Suddenly, Curly and his horse raced through enemy gunfire and arrows and shot two Arapaho warriors. As soon as Curly saw the second warrior fall, he reached down to scalp the man for his war trophy, a symbol of his skills as a warrior. At that moment Curly was shot in the leg! Though he wasn't severely injured, he had learned his lesson: to become the dream rider of his vision, he should not take the scalps of his enemies.

When Curly returned to the Sioux camp, stories were circulating about how he had almost single-handedly won the battle. The whole tribe held a victory dance in his honor. Curly, a quiet boy, downplayed his tremendous role in the battle. To honor his son for his bravery, Curly's father announced to the tribe: "My son . . . has done a brave thing; for this I give him a new name . . . Crazy Horse." For the next seventeen years, Crazy Horse fought in many battles. His reputation as a warrior grew, and he became famous far and wide as a great Sioux leader and war strategist.

> Curly was a great buffalo hunter. He crafted a bow for himself with arrows made of porcupine quills. He located herds by placing his ear to the ground and listening to the thunder of their hooves in the distance. While an experienced hunter was lucky to shoot just one buffalo during a hunt, Curly killed two on his very first trip!

In 1875, a US government commission was sent to meet with the chiefs from several tribes. The commission demanded that the chiefs sign a new treaty that would give almost all of the Sioux, Cheyenne, and Arapaho land to the US government. For three days the chiefs discussed what they should do. When the commission returned, accompanied by 120 US soldiers, they were shocked to discover themselves surrounded by seven thousand warriors. The land negotiations failed, and the result was all-out war.

Though not all the Sioux wanted to fight, Crazy Horse saw no other option. He remembered the death of Conquering Bear, who had been so unfairly shot, and declared, "For me there is no country that can hold the tracks of the moccasin and the boots of the white man side by side." It was time for war. In 1876, Cheyenne forces joined the Sioux to form an army and fight US forces. In one of their first major battles, later called Custer's Last Stand, just forty Indians were killed, compared to the deaths of General Custer and 220 US soldiers. The Sioux strategy was brilliant, combining surprise attacks with detailed knowledge of their land.

> Before each battle, Crazy Horse rubbed dirt all over his body and his horse. He also wore a special stone to protect his heart. He wore the same face paint as the warrior in his vision. All these things were part of Crazy Horse's battle protection, or WO-TA-WE.

This taste of victory didn't last long, however. Outnumbered by the US troops and low on supplies and weapons, the Sioux were in serious trouble. Some warriors fled with their families, but many stayed with Crazy Horse to continue fighting. Unable to get more food or supplies because of the war, many in the tribe grew sick. Crazy Horse, worried for the welfare of his people, made a difficult choice: he decided to surrender.

In 1877, Crazy Horse marched into Fort Robinson with eight hundred followers to give himself up. A group of Sioux, who had surrendered earlier, were waiting for them and sang out in strong voices welcoming their leader. One soldier commented, "By God, this is a triumphal march, not a surrender." Even though they'd lost the battle, the

Sioux were proud they'd stood up and defended their land and their way of life. General Clark, head officer of the fort, shook the hand of the great warrior, and Crazy Horse said, "I have been a man of war and have always protected my country against invaders. Now I am for peace. I will . . . fight no more."

Though most Sioux greatly admired the courageous warrior, a few were jealous and did not like Crazy Horse. They spread rumors that he was planning to murder General Clark. When soldiers arrested him, Crazy Horse tried to escape and was stabbed with a bayonet. That night, at age thirty-six, Crazy Horse died. The next day, soldiers went to bury the body, but Crazy Horse's friend Touch of Clouds pulled a gun on them. Touch of Clouds brought Crazy Horse's body to his father for a traditional Sioux burial. Legend says that every night until Crazy Horse was buried, an eagle paced across his coffin. Crazy Horse's father buried the body, not telling a soul of the grave's location.

> The Crazy Horse monument has been under construction for more than 50 years. The head alone is nine stories high, much larger than the heads of the US presidents on nearby Mount Rushmore.

Up to the very moment of his death, Crazy Horse fought bravely, staying true to his vision and becoming the great Sioux warrior and protector of his people he had always dreamed of being. Today, a memorial to Crazy Horse is being carved out of a mountainside in the Black Hills, a permanent reminder of Crazy Horse's heroic life. Although the carving is not finished yet, nearby is the Indian Museum of North America, where visitors can browse Indian art, artifacts, and presentations on Indian cultures and history.

HOW WILL YOU ROCK THE WORLD?

I will rock the world by becoming an entrepreneur, a filmmaker, a writer, and a motivational speaker. I will direct films and write novels and nonfiction, which will teach people how to better their lives. I will expand my website, Indigo Chef (indigo-chef.com), to educate hundreds of thousands of people about nutrients, diet, exercise, good attitudes, and naturopathic medicine. I will give talks around the world to thousands of people. I will follow in the footsteps of Jim Rohn and continue to advocate his "art of exceptional living" message.

HEZEKIAH CONDRON ☼ AGE 15

Okita Soji

APPROXIMATELY 1844–1868 ◎ SWORDSMAN ◎ JAPAN

There were some who claimed that not even [the master swordsman] Kondo could beat Okita in a match.

—ROMULUS HILLSBOROUGH, JAPANESE HISTORIAN

The bamboo sword flashed by Soji's face, and he dodged just in time. He flicked his own sword and jabbed forward, straight into the sword instructor's chest. "Point!" the referee called out. Twelve-year-old Okita Soji had just beaten the most famed kenjutsu instructor in Japan!

Soji was born in 1844 in Edo, what is now Tokyo, Japan. His father was a samurai, and Soji spent his days dreaming of being as great a sword fighter as his father. But both his parents died before Soji was even nine years old, and he was left looking for a new family. His father's samurai status allowed him to go to the Shieikan, the dojo in Edo. A dojo is a training facility where people study martial arts, like karate and sword fighting, and the Shieikan was run by Kondo Isami, an

45

impressive samurai. Kondo welcomed Soji into the Shieikan and taught him how to fence. Soji apprenticed to Kondo, learning everything there is to know about sword fighting and teaching martial arts, and they became good friends.

After his legendary win against the fencing master, twelve-year-old Soji became an assistant instructor at the Shieikan. Kondo assigned him to teach at the main dojo in Edo as well as in surrounding villages, where dozens of people scrambled to learn from the teenage fencing wizard.

In many Asian cultures, including Japanese, the family name comes first and the given name comes second. So in the Japanese tradition, a typical American name would be written as Smith John.

During all this time, big changes were happening in Japan. For the past 250 years, the country had been divided into small districts, which were protected by sword-fighting samurais. Although there was an emperor, who lived in Kyoto, he didn't really hold power over the country. The districts didn't listen to him, and they ruled themselves. Many of the districts battled with one another because of disagreements between their people or because one district wanted to take the territory of another. Samurais were known for fighting bloody battles in the name of their districts.

Until the mid-1800s, Japan had very little contact with other countries. People just paid attention to what was going on in their own district. If they knew anything of other places, it was only about the bordering districts. But in 1853 Matthew Perry of the US Navy arrived in Edo with several heavily armed ships and a letter from the US president that the Japanese emperor was to sign a treaty with America, which would open the country to foreigners. The nation was divided. Half the people wanted to sign the treaty. The other half wanted to fight the foreigners to keep their country independent and isolated. These people believed opening the country would portray a sign of weakness, and they considered the foreigners to be barbarians who they did not want in their land.

The emperor decided to sign the treaty, but many of the samurais revolted. Even retired samurais who did not fight anymore came back, sharpened their swords, and went to battle against government officials, fighting to keep Japan free of foreigners. The emperor knew he had to do something to stop the rebelling samurais from attacking his palace in Kyoto. He hired a protector of Kyoto, who then hired thirteen of the best swordsmen in the country to subdue the rebels and to restore law and order. This group, which later grew to more than one hundred, was called the Shinsengumi. Kondo Isami was chosen as a commander of the group, and he selected Okita Soji as one of his swordsmen.

The purpose of the Shinsengumi was to protect Kyoto and the emperor, and to make the rebels be peaceful. Two of the Shinsengumi warriors believed themselves to be above the law, though, and they killed whomever they thought was rude or insulting. Mothers on the street, people in restaurants, shop owners—no one was safe. This brought the Shinsengumi a bad reputation, and while their enemies feared and despised them, so did the people they were supposed to be protecting. Soji and many of the other men were upset by this.

The summer of 1864 brought a turn of events, though. The two corrupt men of the Shinsengumi died, and then the Shinsengumi successfully stopped the rebels from burning down the palace. They'd heard about the rebels' plan, but they didn't know where they were hiding. The Shinsengumi caught one of the rebels and questioned him about the hiding place of his teammates. He refused to answer, so the Shinsengumi tied him to a gate, leaving him there until he would cooperate. When a neighbor saw him and untied him, the Shinsengumi were watching and quietly followed him to the rebel

> KENJUTSU—which means the art of the sword—is a kind of sword fighting that is done with a bamboo or wooden sword in a safe place, like a dojo, and in which each opponent gets a point for tapping the other on the head, throat, wrists, or abdomen. People practice KENJUTSU to get better at sword fighting, which is done on the battlefield.

hideout. There, they found one of the rebel leaders and stacks of papers proving the plan to burn the palace down. They also found evidence that the rebels were planning to kidnap the emperor!

It was clear that this was just one of the hideouts, though, so the Shinsengumi questioned the rebel leader until they found out where the other hideouts were. That night, Kondo took Soji and eight others to the Ikéda'ya Inn on the west side of Kyoto. They passed through the Gion Festival, where hundreds of red-and-white lanterns and thousands of people crowded the streets. Outside the gate of the inn, Soji and the other men dressed themselves in chain mail armor and iron helmets. They snuck up to the windows of the inn and could hear the rebels upstairs discussing their plan for the next attack. The rebels grew excited and rowdy, completely unaware that the Shinsengumi was lurking outside. Kondo and Soji snuck in, found the rebels' extra weapons and tied them up, and then yelled for the inn owner.

> Okita Soji had a reputation for killing his enemy in a single move. In nearly every Shinsengumi battle, he is said to have killed at least one person with one swift swipe of his sword.

When the owner came, Kondo announced that the Shinsengumi needed to search the inn. The owner tried to resist, but Kondo and Soji pushed past him and ran up the stairs. They were met by twenty rebels, all with swords drawn. One rushed forward to attack, and Soji killed him in one movement. Frightened, the other rebels rushed downstairs, where they were attacked by the remaining Shinsengumi. Soon, twenty more Shinsengumi showed up and joined the fight. Although Soji collapsed in a coughing fit, spitting up blood, the Shinsengumi were victorious. The next morning, they marched back to the palace while a crowd of thousands cheered from the sides of the roads.

The rebels came back later, fighting even harder, though. The rest of the war proved long and bloody. Kondo was captured and killed on May 17, 1868, and the Shinsengumi was severely weakened. At the end of that month, the Shinsengumi was preparing to head into battle, and Soji wanted to join, but his coughing had grown much worse. At only twenty-five years old, he was dying of tuberculosis. He insisted, "I'll take up my sword to kill the enemy," but he could not. The Shinsengumi continued to fight until May 1869, when they were defeated and a new era of leadership took over in Japan.

Even though the Shinsengumi lost in the end, they fought courageously to protect the emperor and to restore peace in a violent country. Okita Soji is featured in several books, including the manga *Kaze Hikaru* and *Peacemaker Kurogane*, which was turned into a television anime series. He is even one of the main characters in the X-Box video game *Kengo: The Legend of the 9 Samurai*. The digital comic "Okita and the Cat," released for Apple mobile devices in August 2010, portrays Soji during the last days before he died, when he wished he could fight.

ROCK ON!

BARUANI NDUME

In a crowded refugee camp in Tanzania, Baruani Ndume is working to make a difference. He is just one of more than thirty thousand children refugees from the Democratic Republic of Congo in the camp, most of whom, like Baruani, have lost touch with their families. Baruani set up a radio program to help these children cope with their challenges and also to find their families. In 2009 Baruani was presented with the International Children's Peace Prize for his outstanding work.

Thomas Alva Edison

1847–1931 ◈ INVENTOR ◈ UNITED STATES

Genius is one percent inspiration and ninety-nine percent perspiration.

—THOMAS EDISON

When fifteen-year-old Tom walked into the offices of *The Detroit Free Press* to buy the newspapers he would sell later that day, he was met by a worried crowd. It was 1862, and the Civil War Battle of Shiloh was underway. There were vague reports that hundreds of men had been killed. Tom sold papers and snacks on the train between Detroit and Port Huron, Michigan, but the mood in the office gave him a new business idea: people wanted information about the war and he would *sell* it to them.

At the train station, he asked the telegraph operator to wire a bulletin about the Battle of Shiloh to the stationmaster in each town the train would stop at on its way back to Port Huron. Tom asked the stationmasters to write down the battle report on the station blackboard. Then he went back to the newspaper office and convinced them to give him one thousand papers, instead of his usual one hundred, promising to pay them the next day. On the train that day, just as Tom had thought, people read the blackboard bulletins and wanted more information. At first he sold papers to them for five cents, but by the last stop, people were so eager for news that he sold the papers for a quarter each! He sold every paper that day, and he learned a valuable lesson: an idea that is useful to a large number of people can make you money!

Thomas Alva Edison was born in 1847; at birth, his head was so alarmingly big that the doctor said he had a brain fever. Must have been all those brains, because by the time he died, in 1931, Thomas Edison held 1,093 patents for inventions, the most of any American inventor. (A patent is a certificate that gives an inventor exclusive rights to use or sell his or her invention, and it keeps other people from stealing the idea and making money from it.) Two of his most famous inventions were the phonograph (the ancestor of today's CD and MP3 players) and the electric light bulb.

Tom created the world's first invention factory in Menlo Park, New Jersey. The men who worked there were as thrilled to be on the cutting edge of technology as Bill Gates must have been when he invented his first computer operating system!

After that day on the train, when the telegraph helped Tom make money selling newspapers, he was hooked on it. He began working as a telegraph operator in his teens. The telegraph, ancestor of the telephone, was operated by turning an electric switch off and on at different rates to create a clicking sound that was transmitted over a wire. Each letter had its own click sound, and telegraph operators had to translate the clicks into English for the person receiving the message. It was the first electric form of long-distance communication.

The telegraph did have one big downfall, however. It couldn't send a message more than two hundred miles. If a message had to travel more than that, it had to pass through many stations, where each operator listened to the message and then sent it to the next station. With all those people interpreting the clicks, the final message often sounded nothing like the original. (If you've ever played the game Telephone, you understand the problem.) While working as a telegraph operator, Tom made a breakthrough. He fixed a machine so that it could receive a message and send it on automatically. But instead of receiving a reward for this bit of genius, he was fired. His supervisor had been working on the very same problem and wasn't too happy that he'd been upstaged by a nineteen-year-old.

> Tom nicknamed his first two children Dot and Dash after the telegraph signals.
>
> ~~~

But getting fired was no big deal to Tom. He really wanted to spend his time inventing anyway. He began writing down all of his ideas, his experiments, and their results. (When he died, he had filled more than 3,400 notebooks!) Tom was so excited about his many ideas, he wrote, "I am twenty-one. I may live to be fifty. I have got so much to do, and life is so short. I am going to hustle." His first invention was an automatic vote counter. It worked perfectly. The only problem was, no one wanted it. It was the first and last time Tom would work on an invention that people didn't need. Like today's entrepreneurs, he only wanted to invent things that people wanted.

> Tom even invented a primitive photocopier. You wrote with an electric pen on a special sheet of waxed paper. Instead of ink coming out, the pen made tiny holes, turning the paper into a stencil. Then ink was pressed through the stencil to make more copies.
>
> ~~~

Penniless at twenty-one, Tom moved to New York City where his friend Franklin Pope let him sleep in the back room of a Wall Street business. After the workers went home, Tom spent his evenings snooping around until he figured out how all the equipment worked. One day the office exploded in chaos: the ticker machine, which sent minute-by-minute gold prices to clients, had broken. As angry clients crowded into the office, Tom told the frantic boss he could fix the machine. "Fix it! Fix it!" the boss screamed back.

Within hours, Tom had fixed it so that the problem would never happen again. That success encouraged him to open a business with his friend. Pope Edison & Company's motto was to "devise electrical instruments and solve problems to order."

By twenty-three, Tom had already earned tons of money on his improved ticker machine and was on his way to a lifetime of inventions. It wasn't all easy: often in the early years he went broke when an invention didn't work, and he spent over $2 million defending his patents against people who tried to steal them. But by the time he was thirty-nine, he was a millionaire, ready for the most important—and the public's favorite—invention of his life.

In 1876, Alexander Graham Bell invented the telephone. It converted the human voice into electric signals. Then, at the receiving end, the electric signals were converted back into a voice. It was scratchy and hard to hear, but it worked. Tom, of course, wanted to make it better.

While trying to improve the sound quality of the telephone, Tom stumbled upon something else altogether. He used the telephone's diaphragm (a flexible disk that vibrates with the sound of a voice) and a pin to put the sound waves of human speech on paper: "I rigged up an instrument and pulled a strip of the paper through it at the same time shouting, 'Halloo!'" The sound vibrated the diaphragm, causing the pin to mark the paper. Then,

> When Tom worked the midnight shift as a telegraph operator, his boss made him prove he was awake by sending a telegraph every hour. Tom promptly rigged up the machine to automatically signal his boss every 60 minutes, while he snoozed away!

when he pulled the paper through the instrument again, the pin's marks activated another diaphragm. A ghostly "Halloo!" was heard. "I was never so taken aback in all my life," recalled Tom. He had just invented the phonograph—the ancestor of today's MP3 players. You can thank Thomas Edison next time you play your favorite song.

Yeah, music is important, but Tom's next big thing *really* changed the world. Like many other inventors at the time, Tom was obsessed with creating an electric light. He bragged that he would soon be able to light up Lower Manhattan, but it wasn't as easy as he expected. For over a year, he searched for the right material for the filament (the thread-like part of the light bulb that glows), trying different metals and even bamboo fibers. Lucky for Tom, his labs were filled with odd pieces of minerals, plant parts, tools, rocks—just about anything he thought might be useful. Tom believed "the most important part of an experimental laboratory is a big scrap heap." In that scrap heap the perfect filament was finally found.

Back then, oil lamps were used for light; when the lamps burned, they left a black residue, carbon, on their glass globes. Tom was absent-mindedly rolling a bit of this carbon, called lampblack, between his fingers when he suddenly realized it might make good material for the filament. He was right. And the first light bulb was born.

It took three more years for crews to tear up streets and walls in a ten-square-block area of New York City to put in electrical wiring. Although it wasn't quite lighting up all of Lower Manhattan, when Tom threw the switch to turn on eight hundred lights in twenty-five buildings, no one complained! Tom's thoughts on that day: "I have accomplished all I promised." The electric age had begun!

Over the rest of his long life (he lived to be eighty-four years old), Tom continued to work on inventions. Unlike some inventors, whose ideas are known only to experts, Thomas Edison always wanted to make things that were useful to everyone. He was never content to accept things as they appeared—his genius was to find a better use for a machine, or a way for it to work better. His ideas paved the way for the thousands of electronic tools, games, and entertainment systems we have today. Eighty years after his death, his influence is still felt as we live an electrified life, one full of useful inventions that sprang from the brain of Thomas Edison.

HOW WILL YOU ROCK THE WORLD?

I will rock the world by revolutionizing air transportation. I will design an aircraft that can cross any ocean in record-breaking time. I will also design a spacecraft that is cheap and efficient and can fly people into outer space on a regular basis. I have already designed a ship that will travel to Mars!

KWAME ANYIKA ☼ AGE 12

CHesteR GReenwood

1858–1937 ◦ INVENTOR ◦ UNITED STATES

The only practical way to keep the ears from freezing when exposed to such weather as all the northern states are liable to at certain seasons, is to cover them up; but this is easier said than done, or at least it was until Greenwood's Champion Ear Protectors were invented.

—1889 DESCRIPTION OF THE FARMINGTON MANUFACTURING COMPANY IN
LEADING BUSINESS MEN OF LEWISTON, AUGUSTA AND VICINITY

Chester excitedly laced up his new ice skates and glided onto the glassy surface of Abbott Pond. It was an especially cold, windy day in Farmington, Maine, so there were no other children ice skating, but Chester didn't care. He wasn't going to let a little cold weather keep him from trying out his new ice skates.

Before long, though, Chester's ears were stinging with pain from the cold. He hated wearing fur caps—they didn't fit well, and the chin strap made him look like a little boy. He was fifteen, basically a man, and he did not want people to think he was a boy anymore. He rubbed his mittened hands over his ears, but that didn't help. Then he took his scarf off and wrapped it around his head. *This can't look good*, he thought. Besides, the scarf was way too big to be comfortable, and it made his head itch. Defeated, Chester trudged home.

That night, Chester's brain was whirring with ideas to solve his problem. He found a piece of wire and started bending it into an arc that would fit over his head. Then he bent the ends into circles about the size of his ears.

"Grandmother," he said. "Could you sew some fur on this so I can use it as ear protectors?" The first earmuffs had been made!

Chester Greenwood was born in December of 1858 in Maine, where New England winters can be bitingly cold. His father, Zina, built bridges, wagons, and carriages, so Chester and his brothers were constantly inspired to create and build.

From an early age, Chester was a businessperson. He sold the eggs his family's chicken laid and then used the money to buy candy, which he then marked up—raised the price—and sold to his neighbors.

> Even though Chester never finished elementary school, he was a strong supporter of education. All four of his children went to college.
>
> ᴍᴍ

Less than three years after that cold winter's day in 1873, Chester had acquired a patent for Greenwood's Champion Ear Protectors. The patent protected his design so nobody else could use it without paying him. Then he set to work improving his design with an adjustable steel band and hinges so the earmuffs could be folded up and fit in a pocket. He designed machinery to mass produce the earmuffs, and at age twenty-two, Chester made a display about his product and the production process to show at the state fair. Hundreds of people saw his display there, and it paid off not only because he won a medal, but also because by 1883, he was selling thirty thousand pairs of earmuffs a year. Chester continued to sell more and more earmuffs every year until his death in 1937, when he sold four hundred thousand!

Chester's ingenuity didn't stop at ear warmers, though. At that time, steam heating was very popular. Basically, a big furnace called a steam boiler had a fire going in the basement of a building and sent hot steam through pipes up to the all the rooms in the building. The downfall of this system, though, was that it was difficult to control the temperature, and it could be dangerous, sometimes starting fires in the building. Chester produced Florida Boilers, a more effective and safe furnace for steam heating.

Chester was proud to be a Farmington resident and worked to make it a nice place to live. He joined a committee to improve roads in the town, and he and his wife were active in the church, the Grange, and the Odd Fellows lodge. Perhaps most impressive, Chester employed almost a fourth of the town at his factory, Farmington Manufacturing Company.

Many of Chester's inventions weren't patented. He had a reputation in the area for his ability to build machines that solved problems, so often farmers and other folks in the community would come to him when they had a problem. Chester would think about it for a day or two and then build whatever machine was needed to help his friends out. Some of the machines he developed for other companies produced things like rolling pins and tool handles, while others were more complicated, like the wood boring machine. His mousetrap called the Mechanical Cat was in high demand at local hotels, his doughnut hook was perfect for pulling doughnuts out of hot cooking oil, and his shock absorber helped inspire the design for today's airplane landing gear.

In the late 1890s, Chester started Franklin County's first phone company, Franklin Telephone & Telegraph. He even manufactured all the equipment for it! People joked, though, that they had to remove their Greenwood Ear Protectors before they could hear very well on Chester's phone system.

When he was sixty, Chester was tired of the front edge of his tea kettle always wearing out. He, like most people, had a habit of simply tilting the kettle forward to pour water out of the spout and into a cup. This led to extra pressure on that part of the kettle, though, and that's where it always wore out first. Chester decided to fix his problem by adding a leg that extended horizontally out from the bottom of the kettle, under the spout. This supported the kettle as he poured his hot water, and his kettle bottom lasted much longer. When he started selling this product, it—like the earmuffs—was a big hit.

> Every inventor has a list of inventions that didn't succeed. Chester Greenwood's list includes the cotton picker and the advertising match box.

The last invention Chester patented was a spring-tooth rake, made of steel. We still use rakes like this today when we rake grass, sand, and soil.

Though Chester patented 130 inventions—and created many more—he's most remembered for his first, the ear protector. Every year in Farmington, Maine, the whole town salutes Chester's contributions to the community and the country. December 21 is Chester Greenwood Day, and the first Saturday in December is celebrated with a parade in which everyone and everything—even the cars and the animals!—wears earmuffs. The Smithsonian Institute named Chester one of America's fifteen outstanding inventors.

HOW WILL YOU ROCK THE WORLD?

I will rock the world by becoming an architect. I will design bigger, better, and definitely safer buildings. I will design them to help the environment so that they don't pollute the air as much as other buildings do. I also want to be the first person to design underwater living environments so that there won't be as many people crammed onto one continent. I will also design buildings for people who are less fortunate, and I will do my best to listen to other people's ideas when designing new buildings.

KEVIN WALKER ☼ AGE 11

George Washington Carver

APPROXIMATELY 1865–1943 ❊ BOTANIST ❊ UNITED STATES

*It has always been the one great ideal of
my life to be of the greatest good to the
greatest number of "my people" possible.*

—GEORGE WASHINGTON CARVER

The farmer tried everything to get his corn to grow better—more water, different fertilizers—but nothing worked. He was at the end of his rope.

"Take this to the Carver place," he told his son, handing a small, sickly-looking corn stalk to him. "Give it to the Plant Doctor."

The farmer's son had to walk miles to get there, and when he finally found the Plant Doctor, his jaw dropped open in shock. George Washington Carver, dubbed the Plant Doctor by his neighbors, was just eight years old! Yet, when young George took the unhealthy plant, he spoke with great confidence: "Don't worry. I'll put this in my garden and try some things out on it. I'll figure out what's wrong."

When the farmer himself returned to the Carver place a few weeks later, he couldn't believe his eyes. Like magic, his small, wilted corn plant was now tall, green, and healthy. "Here's what you do . . ." and the young scientist described a new kind of fertilizer he'd created that would make the farmer's sick corn grow like crazy. The man shook his head in wonder: *How could a boy know so much about plants?*

Eventually, this eight-year-old Plant Doctor of Missouri would grow up to become the Plant Doctor to the entire United States. His inventions would change the food we eat, and his ideas would help poor farmers grow successful crops and rise from poverty. He would become one of the most famous and respected scientists in the world!

It might be hard to believe, but this scientific genius was actually born into slavery! George Washington Carver and his mother were owned by Moses and Susan Carver. When George was still a baby, he and his mother were kidnapped by greedy Confederate raiders who planned to sell them out of state to the highest bidder. The Carvers offered a reward to get them back, but only George was found. The thieves had left the baby behind when they realized he was sickly. George's mother was never seen again.

> The neighbor who found and returned baby George to the Carvers was given a horse as a reward.

From that day on, the Carvers raised George and his brother, not as slaves, but as their own children. George was small and frail, but he knew that while his body might be scrawny, his brain was brawny. He was fascinated by nature and spent all his free time collecting things to study: plants, rocks, dirt . . . even bugs and frogs. He collected so much that the family built him an outdoor shed to keep it all in. By the time he was eight, George knew so much about nature that his neighbors went to him for advice. He experimented on sick plants in his secret garden in the woods until he made them healthy again.

More than anything, though, George wanted to go to school.

> *When just a mere tot ... my very soul thirsted for an education. I literally lived in the woods. I wanted to know every strange stone, flower, insect, bird, or beast.*

Although everyone in town knew how smart George was, the school for white children wouldn't let him in. Unlike today, when all kids in America—black, white, and every other race—can go to public schools for free, George had no way to learn. Can you imagine wanting to learn so badly that you would walk hundreds of miles, sleep in barns, and work for your food, just to go to *school*? Well, that's exactly what George did when he was only twelve years old! He set out on his own to get an education. He would find a school that would take him, work to pay his way, and learn everything the teachers knew, then take off again to find smarter teachers!

Going to college was George's big dream. It took him years of hard work and travel, but at age thirty he finally finished enough classes and was the first African-American accepted to Iowa State College of Agricultural and Mechanic Arts. Even though he was officially accepted into the college, George still battled fear and prejudice on campus. He was forced to eat meals in the basement instead of in the dining hall with the other students. With quiet dignity, George held his head high, worked hard, and forced the students and faculty to face their racist attitudes.

Before long he was truly accepted everywhere white students went, and

> While George was traveling around getting an education, he lived for a time in a house he built himself ... out of dirt! His sod house was so well built, all the neighbors asked for George's help building theirs.

> Inventor Thomas Edison asked George to be his research partner and offered him a very high salary, but George turned him down because he felt the students at Tuskegee and the farmers in the South needed him more.

he made many friends. At long last the Plant Doctor's dreams came true when he earned his master's degree in agriculture. Though he was offered many teaching jobs at white colleges, George chose to teach at the Tuskegee Normal and Industrial Institute in Alabama, a college for African-Americans. Their Agriculture Department didn't even exist before George arrived, so he and his students had to build everything from scratch, including their classroom! George taught his students to reuse everything they found—discarded bottles became beakers, and jar lids were melted down for chemicals to experiment with. Their department supplied all the food for the entire school, so they quickly learned the most efficient, cheapest ways to grow and manage their plants and animals.

George teaches farmers to recycle! At Tuskegee, George was thrilled to continue some of the research he started as a boy. All around him he saw problems facing poor farmers, so he put his brain to work fixing them. Many farmers couldn't afford fertilizer, so George taught them to put their dead plants into a big pile, which eventually rotted down into free fertilizer! Nowadays we call this compost. You may even have a compost pile at *your* house. Feeding farm animals was also expensive, so George invented animal food made from acorns, which grow plentifully in the South and can be collected for free.

George saves the soil! The Plant Doctor helped farmers even more with his discoveries about cotton. This was the main crop grown in the South back then, but it quickly sucked up all the nutrients in the soil. After a few years of growing cotton, farmers couldn't grow anything anymore in their exhausted fields. George discovered that certain plants actually put nutrients back into the soil. He taught farmers to use crop rotation, planting cotton one year, then a crop like peanuts, soybeans, or sweet potatoes the next, to put nutrients back into the soil and make their fields healthy again.

Peanuts were brought to America from Africa with the slaves, who called them goobers. Peanuts were used mostly to feed animals; humans didn't think much of eating them until George came along.

~~~

The US government was so impressed with George's achievements, officials named a submarine after him and put his face on a stamp and the half-dollar.

—᭝᭝᭝—

George goes crazy with peanuts! The farmers didn't know what to do with these strange new crops, so George did some more experiments and invented over three hundred uses for the peanut! He made peanut milk, butter, coffee, shampoo, dye, paint, paper, plastic, and even chop suey sauce! Then he invented a hundred ways to use the sweet potato—everything from chocolate to paste to ink. Thanks to George, everyone uses crop rotation now, and peanuts, sweet potatoes, and soybeans are three of the most popular and profitable crops in the South!

George's ideas became so popular that soon farmers, black and white, from all over the South, were asking his advice. His reputation spread quickly, and in 1918, the US government invited him to the capital to tell them about his ideas. His brilliant work was starting to make him famous, and he won tons of awards ... even from beyond the grave! In 1990, almost fifty years after he died, George became the first African-American to be inducted into the National Inventors Hall of Fame.

Even with all the fame, George preferred the simple life. Unlike many scientists today, who make millions when they patent their inventions, George never asked for or earned *any* money from his many discoveries. He believed his ideas were given to him by God and should be shared with others for free. If people sent him checks for his help, he returned them. George worried that if he earned lots of money, he would get so busy taking care of the money that he wouldn't have time for research. He was so devoted to science

George had many passions. He loved art so much that he almost gave up science to become a painter. He painted on everything—cans, scraps of paper, the walls, the floor. One of his paintings, YUCCA AND CACTUS, was even displayed at the 1893 World's Fair in Chicago.

—᭝᭝᭝—

that he never married either. When asked why, George answered, "How could I explain to a wife that I have to go outdoors at four o'clock every morning to talk to the flowers?" He was quite happy with his research, knowing he was helping the world.

Henry Ford, inventor of the assembly line, was such an admirer of George that he built a school and a museum named after him.

George continued his teaching and research at Tuskegee up until the day he died in 1943. At his funeral, President Franklin Roosevelt sadly remarked, "The world of science has lost one of its most eminent figures . . . his genius and achievement [were] truly amazing." So, next time you eat a peanut-butter-and-jelly sandwich or spread fertilizer over your garden, maybe you'll think of the young Plant Doctor and his unstoppable dreams.

ROCK ON!

AKRIT JASWAL

Akrit Jaswal enrolled in school at age five and found it far too easy—within a year, he was teaching the classes! Bored with Shakespeare, he began building a library of medical texts, and the doctors at the hospitals in his town in India started letting him observe their surgical procedures. When a poor family came to Akrit needing help, the seven-year-old agreed to operate on their daughter for free. The surgery was a success, and Akrit headed to Punjab University, becoming the youngest student to attend college in the history of India.

Matthew Alexander Henson

1866–1955 ❁ EXPLORER ❁ UNITED STATES

No other but a Peary party would have attempted to travel in such weather. Our breath was frozen to our hood of fur and our cheeks and noses frozen.

—MATTHEW A. HENSON, *A NEGRO EXPLORER AT THE NORTH POLE*

Matt's eyes widened as he neared the shipyard in Baltimore. He'd memorized every word of the stories Baltimore Jack told him in the restaurant back in Washington, DC.

But this day was quiet. Matt could see the mastheads of a ship swaying and bobbing over the warehouses as he wandered along the cobblestone streets toward the water. Finally, he rounded the last corner and saw the ship from bow to stern. The three tall masts were nearly covered in a complex pattern of ropes and yardarms. But what drew Matt's eye was the gold lettering at the front of the ship: *Katie Hines*.

Matt's eyes lingered for a moment longer on the shiny black hull of the ship, and then he scanned the rest of the shipyard. A man sat unmoving near the ship, as mesmerized with it as Matt was. As Matt drew closer to the old man, he asked, "Is this your ship?"

"That she is, son," the man answered, and Matt could feel his own chest swell with excitement at the sound of the pride in the man's voice.

Before long, Captain Childs had hired the young African-American to be the cabin boy on the *Katie Hines*, never imaging that Matthew Alexander Henson would make history.

Matt was born in 1866 in his parents' cabin in Charles County, Maryland. They were sharecroppers, freeborn African-Americans after slavery was outlawed in the United States, and they farmed a small lot of land behind the cabin. When Matt was just three years old, his mother died.

> Janey was so nice to Matt, he thought of her kind of like a mom. He called her Aunty Janey, and when he decided to go to sea, he was very worried he would hurt her feelings.
>
> ~~~

As if that wasn't bad enough, his father remarried a woman who beat Matt and his brothers and sisters. After his father died in 1874, Matt couldn't take his stepmother's beatings anymore, and he ran away to Washington, DC.

In Washington, Matt looked for work. It was hard—even though slavery was over, people were still cruel to blacks. Then he found Janey's Home-Cooked Meals Café. When Janey Moore saw the dirty eleven-year-old boy with worn-out clothes, she smiled and took him in. She gave him food, clothes, and a job in the café. Matt worked hard, and Janey paid him fairly.

Matt's favorite customer at the café was Baltimore Jack. The old man had been a slave on a plantation in New Orleans, and when the plantation owner's son decided to run away from home so he could search for sunken treasure in the sea, he took Jack with him. Before long, Jack's young master got in a knife fight and lost his life, leaving Jack a free man. For many years after that, Jack worked on merchant vessels and, as he told Matt, lived the exciting life of a sailor.

Now face-to-face with a real captain and his first job aboard a ship, Matt shivered with excitement. As the cabin boy, Matt did whatever Captain Childs told him to do—from fetching something to drink to knotting loose ropes and washing the deck. And Captain Childs told Matt to study too. He could see the boy had never been to school, and he taught Matt to read and write, instructing him in math, literature, and navigation.

The life of a sailor—or at least, a cabin boy—was not as exciting as Baltimore Jack had made it out to be, though, and when Captain Childs died, Matt decided to head back to dry land for a job. Only two years later, Matt was pining for the sea again when he met Navy Lieutenant Robert Peary, who was about to sail to Nicaragua for a canal route survey. Seeing nineteen-year-old Matthew Henson's dexterity and learning of his experience at sea, Peary hired Matt as his servant to help with the trip. Matt would quickly prove his intelligence, and Peary continued to hire Matt for seven more expeditions—never again just as his servant.

From 1891 to 1909, Peary and Matthew, along with their crew, explored the Arctic. During their second expedition, the team stood at a viewpoint overlooking a cape in Northwest Greenland. Peary, out of fondness for his friend and fellow explorer, named it Cape Henson.

The most famous expedition of Robert Peary and Matthew Henson would be their last one together. They had already explored farther north than anybody ever had before, but they were determined to reach the North Pole. On August 18, 1909, Peary and Matthew boarded a ship named *Roosevelt* along with forty-nine people from an Inuit village, 246 dogs, seventy tons of whale meat, guns and other hunting equipment, and coal.

In February they dropped anchor near the polar ice cap in the Arctic. The team loaded up the sleds with food and blankets, harnessed the sled dogs, and headed into the icy wilderness. It was not an easy path, though. The ice froze in rough formations, making it hard to pass over it. The crew had to pound at the ice with pickaxes to clear a path. In some places, the thick ice split as they were going over it, making the loudest and most frightening cracking sound Matthew had ever heard. Whenever this would happen, they'd have to adjust their route so they wouldn't be in danger of falling through the ice into the frigid Arctic Ocean.

By March, the sleds were not always together. Matthew found himself amid a vast white landscape with only his sled dogs for company. Determined to find the North Pole, he focused on his navigation equipment and encouraged the dogs to run faster. When he reached the coordinates of the North Pole, Matthew almost cried with joy—or maybe he would have if it hadn't been so cold that his tears would have frozen on his face! Forty-five minutes later, Peary's sled arrived.

"I think I'm the first man to sit on top of the world," Matthew said proudly. But to Matthew's surprise, Peary did not share in his excitement.

Instead, Peary quietly focused on fastening the flag to the pole he'd brought. The rough way he tied the knots and jammed the pole into the snow revealed anger. After years of planning and leading expeditions, he wanted to be the first man to reach the North Pole. Peary felt that Matthew was claiming the glory that was rightfully his, and their friendship would never be the same.

Matthew Henson and the Inuit people were good friends. They called him Matthew the Kind One, and he even had a son, Anaquak, with a woman from the Inuit village.

The argument about who was the first man to the North Pole raged for years. While Peary accepted several awards within the next few years for his work on the expedition, Matthew would not receive the recognition he deserved for a long time. Matthew wrote his account of the expedition, called *A Negro Explorer at the North Pole*, which was published in 1912, and Peary wrote several books too. It was clear, though, that Matthew's time on Peary's team of explorers had ended, so when President Taft offered him a clerk position in the New York Customs House in 1913, Matthew accepted it. He held that position for twenty-three years. While Matthew worked for the government, he also attended Harvard and earned a master's degree.

In 1937, when Matthew was seventy years old, he finally began to receive recognition for his work on the 1909 expedition. The Explorers Club in New York awarded him an honorary membership, and then in 1944 he accepted a Congressional silver medal. In 1954, President

Eisenhower honored Matthew at the White House. Even after Matthew died in 1955, America continued to honor him. In 1998, the Navy named the USNS *Henson* after him, and in 2000, National Geographic honored him with the prestigious Hubbard Award.

Throughout Matthew Henson's life, hard work, fairness, and honesty were important to him. From the small restaurant in Washington, DC, to the final Arctic expedition, Matthew gave his all. It's a good thing he was finally rewarded for it.

HOW WILL YOU ROCK THE WORLD?

I want to rock the world by being the world's greatest globetrotting photojournalist and athlete of all time! I was born in Barcelona, Spain. I have traveled to many places and taken many pictures with my dad's professional camera during my journeys. Although I enjoy photography and would like a career in this area, sports—namely basketball—is my first true love. I am already 6'1" tall, and I play ball every day. One day I hope to play basketball professionally like my father and take plenty of pictures while I am doing so!

REGINALD JOHNSON JR.　AGE 12

Pablo Picasso

1881–1973 ❖ ARTIST ❖ SPAIN

Every child is an artist. The problem is how to
remain an artist once he grows up.

—PABLO PICASSO

Fifteen-year-old Pablo looked up from his easel. The bowl of grapes he was painting seemed to stare back at him. Rubbing his eyes, Pablo examined his still life painting: each grape was supposed to look perfectly realistic, but instead they just looked flat and lifeless on his canvas. He wanted to capture how the fruit *really* looked . . . but how? The rest of the day, Pablo experimented with various brush strokes until he finally came up with a new technique he was happy with.

That evening, Pablo's father, José Ruiz, a well-known painter and art teacher, returned home from his classes. José was most famous for his paintings of pigeons—in fact, most people thought he was the best pigeon painter in all of Spain! "Did you complete your painting, Pablito?" José asked.

Pablo nodded, nervously pointing to the still life drying in the studio. What would his father think of his new technique? José only stared in amazement at Pablo's work. *What's wrong?* Pablo wondered. Finally José said, "My son, you have surpassed my talents—I can no longer paint in the shadow of such work."

From that day on, Pablo's father stopped painting completely. His son Pablo, however, would go on to paint many more masterpieces . . . most of them not in the realistic style José so greatly admired. Unlike most artists, who become famous only after they die, Pablo Picasso would enjoy great fame while he was still alive. His paintings would revolutionize the art world and be celebrated worldwide!

> Picasso was truly a starving artist when he first arrived in Paris. He had almost no food or furniture, so Picasso painted the walls of his studio with everything he wanted—tables piled with delicious food, a huge soft bed . . . even servants!

Painting may have come easily for Pablo Picasso, but he faced many struggles in his early years. Born on October 25, 1881, in Malaga, Spain, Pablo was horribly shy as a child and a real underachiever. Even though he didn't excel socially or academically, his mother, María, told him, "If you become a soldier, you'll be a general; if you become a monk, you'll end up as the pope." Whatever Pablo's career in life, she was sure he would achieve greatness.

Because his father was an art teacher, Pablo was introduced to painting at an early age. When he was only ten, he completed his first major painting, revealing a talent well beyond his years. By the time Pablo was fourteen, he took the entrance exam for the Academy of Fine Arts in Barcelona. For older students, the grueling exam took at least a month, but Pablo finished it in just one day.

While at the academy, Pablo excelled in his work and refined his painting technique, but was unhappy with his teachers' narrow-mindedness when it came to art. At fourteen, Pablo painted *The Old Fisherman*. Because the painting was not *exactly* realistic, Pablo's instructors disapproved. Pablo changed art schools and by age sixteen was winning praise and honors, but his style was still criticized as being too different. Pablo was not happy. He wanted to express himself freely!

Frustrated with his painting career in Spain, nineteen-year-old Pablo moved to Paris. Paris was the center of the art world, a place where artists could break away from traditional styles. Pablo blossomed, exploring abstract styles of painting. If he saw a painting he liked, he would try to copy the artist's style and learn from it. Soon he was able to reproduce the techniques and styles of famous painters like Degas and Monet, but he still hadn't found his *own* artistic style.

> During his Rose Period, Picasso so loved the circus that he went three or four times a week!
> ~~~

Pablo's artistic breakthrough finally came by way of a tragedy: his best friend committed suicide. Pablo went into a deep depression, and his art reflected his mood. He began painting people on the edge of society—beggars, prostitutes, the physically disabled—using mostly blue and gray colors. The paintings were unique and totally different from anything Pablo had done before. This time period, from 1901 to 1903, is now called Picasso's Blue Period.

Pablo's paintings changed again in 1904, this time thanks to love. He met Fernande, a beautiful, red-haired artist's model. As his grief lifted with this new relationship, Pablo started painting in pink, rose, and earth tones instead of dark, depressing colors. He also focused on a new subject matter: colorful circus performers and other artists like himself. This was later called Picasso's Rose Period.

> One of Picasso's most famous cubist sculptures is in downtown Chicago. Built in 1967, the gigantic steel sculpture is 50 feet tall, and some art critics believe that Picasso used his dog as the model for it!
> ~~~

As his work was gaining fans in Paris, Pablo started exploring other creative techniques. Instead of using color to make his paintings different, he studied African art and experimented with geometric shapes. From these forms emerged the style that Pablo is now famous for: cubism. People were shocked by Pablo's wild new paintings, which were so abstract it was hard to tell what was going on. They looked as if they had been shattered, like glass, and then put back together the wrong way. Though many people criticized the strange new paintings, others marveled at Pablo's creativity. Cubism was soon the talk of the town. Demand for Pablo's work grew quickly, and it wasn't long before his paintings were worth thousands, then millions, of dollars!

Even though Pablo is most famous for cubism, he continued to experiment with his style throughout his life. A prolific painter, Pablo would sometimes paint three or four masterpieces in a single day. He created thousands of works of art, including paintings, stage set designs, book illustrations, sculptures, ceramics, prints, and collages. One of his most famous paintings was *Guernica*, which Pablo painted in 1937 to protest the cruelty of the Spanish Civil War. To Pablo, art was his way of fighting society's injustices.

Pablo painted until the end of his life, finishing one final self-portrait just before he died at the age of ninety-one. The son of a painter of pigeons, Pablo grew up to be one of the wealthiest and most praised artists in the world. From the highly realistic work of his youth to his more famous cubist paintings, Pablo has inspired art lovers like no one else.

ROCK ON!

CHRIS COLFER

Most people know actor Chris Colfer as Kurt Hummel on *Glee*, but his talent is far-reaching. When Chris was fourteen, he assistant-directed a play at a hospital fund-raiser. In high school, he wrote, directed, and starred in musicals, so it's no surprise the casting supervisors of *Glee* noticed his talent. In 2011, Chris won a best actor award from the Hollywood Foreign Press Association (HFPA) and was nominated for Outstanding Performance by a Male Actor in a Comedy Series at the 2011 Screen Actors Guild Awards. He recently sold the rights to the movie he wrote, *Struck by Lightning*.

Albert Einstein

1879–1955 ❋ PHYSICIST ❋ SWITZERLAND AND UNITED STATES

Imagination is more important than knowledge.
Knowledge is limited.
Imagination encircles the world.

—ALBERT EINSTEIN

Albert took a breath of fresh mountain air as he walked up the steep slope. Ahead of him was Professor Winteler, one of the few teachers Albert liked, and several classmates. Professor Winteler often took his students on hikes in the Swiss Alps. Staring at the sunlight reflecting off the snowy hills, Albert's mind drifted. *What would it be like if people could travel at the speed of light?* he wondered. Lost in thought and not paying attention to the path, Albert suddenly tripped and slid toward the edge of a cliff! Just before tumbling down the mountain, Albert grabbed on to some icy rocks, and a friend reached out to him with his walking stick.

"Thanks!" Albert said, grabbing the stick. "You saved my life!"

It wasn't the first time scientific questions had distracted Albert Einstein, and it wouldn't be the last. Later that same year, sixteen-year-old Albert wrote his first scientific paper titled *On the Investigation of the State of Ether in the Magnetic Field*. The paper brought up questions that were burning in Albert's mind and that many scientists had never considered before. It paved the way for his future as one of the most remarkable scientists in human history, a man whose theories would transform the way we perceive the universe.

When Albert Einstein was born in Ulm, Germany, in 1879, the first thing his grandmother said was that he was "much too fat! Much too fat!" Albert's head seemed abnormally large, and his family was worried there might be something seriously wrong with him. But Albert grew up to be a healthy and fairly normal young boy. His father, Hermann Einstein, sold feather beds for a living, and his mother, Pauline, cared for Albert and his little sister, Maja. Albert's mother encouraged him to explore and question the world as much as possible. At five, Albert was given a compass to play with while recovering from an illness. Fascinated by the needle's movements, Albert realized that there was some force making the needle point always in the same direction. Suddenly he realized there was "something deeply hidden . . . behind things."

Albert's curiosity ruled him, but it also made it difficult for him to concentrate in school. He would constantly daydream about nature's hidden forces. When he spoke in class, his teachers thought he talked too slowly. Soon they began calling him *Herr Langweil*,

> Einstein's Theory of Relativity came to the shocking conclusion that time, weight, and mass are not constant. When moving at high speeds, all of these things get compressed; only the speed of light remains the same. That happens because energy is equal to mass times the speed of light squared, or $E=mc^2$.

> In his free time, Einstein loved to play the violin and to sail.

which translated means "Mister Stupid." Even the principal said that Albert wouldn't amount to anything. But for Albert, it was nearly impossible to pay attention in class, which consisted mainly of memorizing facts—kids weren't even allowed to ask questions!

Then, one day, a family friend gave Albert a geometry book to read, and his life changed forever. In a short time, twelve-year-old Albert had read the entire book and finished all of its equations. Soon Albert was reading as many science books as he could get his hands on, books like *Force and Matter* and *Kosmos*. By the time Albert was thirteen, he had finished *A Critique on Pure Reason* by Immanuel Kant, a complicated theoretical book that even some professors had a hard time understanding. According to one family friend, "Kant's works, incomprehensible to ordinary mortals, seemed clear to [Albert]." Although Albert's teachers still considered him an idiot, it was becoming apparent to the Einsteins that their son had a unique perspective on the world.

Though Einstein was admired for his intelligence, he was also extremely absentminded: he constantly lost his keys, his clothes never matched or fit right, and he would even forget to eat!

Albert struggled through high school but finally graduated and entered a technical school in Switzerland. At twenty-one, he finished his degree but couldn't get a teaching position, so he eventually settled for a job at the Swiss Patent Office. Albert liked the work because he could learn about new inventions and spend his free time thinking about physics. He did a lot of thinking during his first three years at the patent office and came up with his now-famous Theory of Relativity (otherwise known as $E=mc^2$). The theory had to do with such enormous concepts as how humans understand time, space, and reality. Einstein's idea was radical, and it completely tossed out other established theories.

The scientific community was astounded. How could a lowly patent clerk come up with such a revolutionary theory in physics? Even though Einstein's theory was controversial, his brilliance was finally being recognized. He was offered and accepted a professorship first in Prague,

Czechoslovakia, and then in Berlin, Germany, and was the youngest person ever invited to the world physics conference in Belgium. Einstein enjoyed teaching, and professors and students traveled from across Europe to hear him lecture. By 1919, Einstein's career was skyrocketing. That year, scientists in England proved Einstein's theory correct! News of the discovery circled the globe, and Einstein became world famous. In 1922 he was awarded the Nobel Prize in physics. What his elementary school teachers must have thought!

> Television and fluorescent lights came from Einstein's discovery of the Photoelectric Effect, a theory that proved that light could act like waves and particles.

But physics wasn't Einstein's only passion. He was also a pacifist—a person who believes fighting wars is wrong. Living in Europe, he had witnessed the devastation of World War I and could sense that a second World War was brewing in Germany. He protested against the German government, but to no avail. Hitler and the Nazi Party, racist and political extremists, were gaining more control over the country and limiting the rights of Jewish citizens. Einstein, who was Jewish, feared for his life. (Indeed, by the end of the war, the Nazis had killed millions of Jews.) He fled to the United States in 1933, where he joined the Institute for Advanced Study at Princeton, New Jersey.

By 1939, Hitler had invaded neighboring Poland, and World War II was under way. Einstein was worried that the Nazis would use his theory, $E=mc^2$, to create an atomic weapon that would help them win the war. He wrote to President Franklin Roosevelt, recommending that the United States fund research on atomic weapons. As a pacifist, this must have been a difficult decision for Einstein to make, but the threat of a world ruled by the Nazis terrified him even more. President Roosevelt agreed, and

> The 99th element in the periodic table was discovered shortly after Einstein's death—they named it Einsteinium.

a group of physicists began working on the Manhattan Project, a top-secret mission to create an atomic bomb.

Though Einstein's formula $E=mc^2$ was key to the project, he was not directly involved. In August 1945, America dropped atomic bombs on Hiroshima and Nagasaki, Japan (Germany's ally). The bombings certainly ended the war, but they also killed over a hundred thousand innocent Japanese civilians. Einstein never got over the use of the bombs, and for the rest of his life, he advocated for peace. He declared: "Peace cannot be kept by force; it can only be achieved by understanding."

During his life, Einstein was also part of the Zionist political movement, which wanted to form a new nation for people of Jewish descent. The group's efforts resulted in the creation of the country Israel in 1948. In 1952, Israeli President Chaim Weizmann died, and Israel offered the presidency to Einstein! Though Einstein was honored, he declined, explaining that he was too old and inexperienced for the job.

Three years later, Einstein died from heart failure. Near his bed were several unfinished equations. What was Einstein trying to figure out in those last equations? We may never know. What we do know is that Einstein was one of the world's most remarkable men—a physics genius, an advocate for peace, and a Jewish role model and leader. But to all this, Einstein would probably say, as he said before, "I have no special gift.... I am only passionately curious."

HOW WILL YOU ROCK THE WORLD?

My dream is to be a magnificent biologist who would study the dynamics of life. I will research how living cells work, live, and reproduce and their environment. My inspirations are Bill Nye and Albert Einstein, and I wish I could be like either of these marvelous scientists. Two of the things I want to accomplish as a biologist are to stop animal AIDS and to find a new, unknown organism.

LUCAS SPRAGUE ☼ AGE 12

José Raúl Capablanca

1888–1942 ◎ CHESS PLAYER ◎ CUBA

His technique was flawless, and his style so graceful
and elegant as to make chess look easy. No player
in all the world's history has equalled in artistry,
logic, and crystalline clarity the masterpieces
produced by Capablanca.

—IRVING CHERNEV, BIOGRAPHER

José took a deep breath. This match could mean the beginning of a career for him if he finished well. He'd already played eleven games against Juan Corzo, the defending chess champion of Cuba. Juan easily won the first two, but when the third game was a draw—the technical term for a tie in chess—José realized he might have a chance. Even though Juan had studied the masters and read all the books on chess, José had an intuitive understanding of the game. While Juan had memorized all the tricks a player can do, José could just look at the board and see them.

Now, José had won three games and just needed to win one more. He focused on the board and all the pieces on it.

"Checkmate," José said as he moved his rook, cornering his opponent's king.

The crowd remained silent until the judge examined the chess board and nodded. Then the room erupted with applause. Twelve-year-old José Raúl Capablanca had just become Cuba's national chess champion!

José was born in 1888 in Havana, Cuba. His father enjoyed playing chess, and José often watched. When José was four years old, he giggled during a game his father was playing with a friend. When his father asked him why he was giggling, he responded, "Because you moved your knight to an incorrect square." When his father looked at the board again, he saw that his son was right.

José is often called the Human Chess Machine.

José's father recognized his son's natural talent, so he began taking José to the Central Chess Club of Cuba. There, the best players in the club couldn't defeat little José. He was a genius!

In his teens, José began to think about college, and he decided to move to the United States so he could attend Columbia University in New York City. He took his studies seriously, but he took chess even more seriously, and he spent much of his time with the Manhattan Chess Club, where he built friendships that would last a lifetime. His fellow club members were so impressed with José's abilities that they arranged a tour across the United States for him to play matches against the leading chess players in the country. Near the end of this tour, when José was twenty years old, he went head-to-head with the American chess champion, Frank Marshall, whom he beat 8–1, with fourteen draws. The world was in awe.

In 1911 the chess world prepared for the San Sebastian international tournament in Spain—the most important competition of the year. All the world's best players would be there, with the only exception being World Champion Emanuel Lasker. This tournament had strict qualification guidelines. José did not quite meet them, but Marshall knew José deserved to be there. He insisted the administration allow

José to play, and they did, but whispers were already gathering among the chess community. *What kind of a player expects the rules to be bent for him?* One of the other players, Aron Nimzovich, even told José that he shouldn't talk in the presence of better players. José challenged the man to a series of lightning games—and easily beat him. No one else dared tell José to be quiet. Everyone played their best, and José beat them all. This time, though, there was no grand applause like there had been back in Cuba. Instead, his European rivals said José was just an inexperienced player who got lucky.

But José didn't care. He knew he was an outstanding chess player, and he traveled around Europe playing chess matches in dozens of cities. Then he set his sights on the next title: world champion. Lasker, the current world champion, hadn't come to San Sebastian, but José wanted to play him anyway. He challenged Lasker to a match. Lasker agreed, but only if José met seventeen conditions. José did not agree with several of the conditions, so the two men did not play.

Two years later, José's hometown of Havana hosted a chess tournament to show off its pride for José. He played reasonably well during the tournament, and the championship rested on the final match between José and Marshall, the former American chess champion. Both men wanted the title badly, and they fidgeted with anxiety. Marshall just barely beat José, who felt he had let his country down.

Cuba still supported José whole-heartedly, though, and in 1913, the government appointed José to work in the Cuban Foreign Office. His only job duty was to play chess—they wanted him to represent Cuba well in the upcoming St. Petersburg international chess tournament in 1914. There, he would play against Marshall, Nimzovich, and finally Lasker.

> Lightning chess—also called speed chess, rapid transit chess, or blitz chess—is a fast game in which players have either ten seconds to play each turn or five minutes to play the whole game.

José started out shaky in the first two games of the tournament, but then he gained his strength and eventually met with Lasker to battle for the championship. The two great chess players challenged each other with brutal attacks and sneaky tricks. José fought hard, but Lasker beat him. José still could not call himself the world champion.

Shortly after the St. Petersburg tournament, World War I broke out, putting international chess tournaments on hold. José continued to travel and play chess matches through his position in the Cuban Foreign Office, though, and he was on such a strong winning streak that he started to think he was invincible. Meanwhile, Lasker was working to better the chess profession, arguing that winning chess players deserved to be paid. This was a tough goal, though. By the time the war was over and José was again challenging Lasker for the title of world champion, Lasker had not made any progress in convincing people to pay chess payers, and although he accepted José's challenge, he had little interest in defending his title. He gave up and told José, "You have earned the title."

> The highest compliment a modern chess player can receive is to be told he plays like Capablanca.

Chess fans were sorely disappointed by this lack of sportsmanship, and a year later, José challenged Lasker again. To make the match more appealing to Lasker, though, José convinced sponsors to pay José and Lasker each $12,500 to play the match. Lasker agreed, but after José won four games and there had been ten draws, Lasker gave up again. José was the reigning world champion.

As the chess world continued to grow and change, the world's best players met to discuss new rules. Because José had raised $25,000 to challenge Lasker for the world championship, he believed all future challengers should have to raise at least $10,000. Over the next few years, several players challenged José for his title, but only one was able to raise the money to actually have the match. Alexander Alekhine had the support of the Argentinean government and several businesspeople to challenge José. But then José made another rule—before Alekhine could be considered a challenger, he had to play in a New York tournament. Alekhine was furious that José was making it so hard to challenge him for the title, but he did it anyway.

The world champion match between José and Alekhine finally took place in Buenos Aires, Argentina, in 1927. To win it, one player just had to win six games. It seems simple, but that match ended up being the longest world championship match in history, lasting seventy-three days! After thirty-four games, Alekhine had finally won six games, and he was the new world champion.

In 1942 José was watching a match at the Manhattan Chess Club when he suddenly collapsed. He was rushed to the hospital, but he died the next day.

Although José Raúl Capablanca never won the world champion title back, he is still considered by many to be the greatest chess player of all time. Throughout his career, he played nearly six hundred games, and he only lost thirty-six. Even Alekhine called him "the greatest genius of chess."[5]

ROCK ON!

STEVEN PURUGGANAN

What can you do with twelve plastic cups and about six seconds? Sport stacking! Steven Purugganan discovered the sport when he happened upon the championship on television. He picked up his own set of stacking cups and got to practicing—he was determined to be the best. At age eleven, he won the World Sport Stacking Championship, and then he did it again at ages twelve and thirteen. He holds several Guinness World Records too. His quick hands have earned him media attention from *Time* magazine, ESPN, *The Ellen DeGeneres Show*, and *Extreme Makeover: Home Edition*, as well as a couple commercial gigs from Firefox and McDonald's. As an ambassador of the sport, Steven has traveled around the United States, Asia, and Europe to promote this amazing skill that both kids and adults enjoy.

Salvatore Ferragamo

1898–1960 ◇ SHOE DESIGNER ◇ ITALY AND UNITED STATES

As a designer [Salvatore Ferragamo] has made an indelible mark on the fashion and entertainment industry, creating timeless, classic designs since the 1920s worn the world over by Hollywood's elite.

—LINDA J. BRISKMAN, BEVERLY HILLS MAYOR, PRESENTING
THE RODEO DRIVE AWARD TO SALVATORE FERRAGAMO

*S*alvatore smiled as he held the shoes up to the light. His sister would look lovely at her confirmation ceremony the next day. Then his eye caught a droplet of glue seeping out from between the cardboard sole and the piece of canvas he'd used for the toe. He carefully angled his tool to scrape off the adhesive without scuffing the white canvas. There, now they were perfect. Though the materials were basic, the shoes were stylish and comfortable.

The next day, nine-year-old Salvatore watched proudly as his sister strode confidently and gracefully down the aisle of the church. He wondered if other people in the congregation were admiring his handiwork, and at that moment he knew, without a doubt, that his passion in life was to design and craft shoes.

Salvatore Ferragamo was born in 1898 in Bonito, Italy, a small town about sixty-four miles from Naples. He was the eleventh of fourteen children, and though his parents were full of love, the family was poor. When four of Salvatore's older brothers left for America with dreams of striking it rich, they wanted him to go with them. But Salvatore wasn't ready yet. First he wanted learn the art and science of shoemaking by apprenticing with a shoemaker in Naples. Then, at thirteen, he opened his own shoe shop in his parents' house in Bonito.

His brothers wrote from America with news that they had found work in Boston; one was even working in a boot factory! Salvatore was intrigued by the idea of mass producing shoes. So far, all the shoes he'd made had been produced by hand, which took time. Learning to manufacture hundreds or even thousands of shoes at one time seemed to be the way of the future. He started saving his money, and by fourteen, he had a ticket to America, where he would join his brothers.

The factory was disappointing for Salvatore, though. While the machinery was fascinating, the boots were far from comfortable—heavy, stiff, and awkwardly shaped—and Salvatore realized the true value of handcrafted shoes. He wanted to make shoes that were comfortable *and* stylish.

While working on the East Coast, Salvatore watched the West Coast become a major hot spot of America. The movie business was booming. The first movie studio in Hollywood opened in 1911, and by 1919, Salvatore

There were six pairs of ruby slippers for filming THE WIZARD OF OZ. The pair actress Judy Garland danced in had felt bottoms so they wouldn't make noise on the yellow brick road. Four pairs still exist today—one is at the Smithsonian, and one is displayed at the Disney MGM Studio. The third pair was sold in 2000 for $666,000, and the fourth pair was stolen from the Judy Garland Museum in 2005. Who knows where they are now?

knew that was where he wanted to be. Who better to design and make shoes for than movie stars? He bought a shoe repair shop in Santa Barbara, California, and soon upgraded to a shop in Hollywood, where he became known as the Shoemaker for the Stars. Some of his clients included Audrey Hepburn, Eva Perón, and Marilyn Monroe. He even made the famous ruby slippers for the movie *The Wizard of Oz*!

Salvatore's shoes were truly an art form. He used colors in ways no one else did, and he reshaped the idea of the heel. While other designers were sticking with the standard pump heel, Salvatore made platforms, cage heels, wedges, and stilettos. In one design, he was inspired by recent archaeological finds in Egypt, and the shoe heel is shaped like an upside-down pyramid!

But Salvatore thought he could do better. The stars loved the shoes he designed and made—they were fashionable and unique—but his shoes still weren't known for being comfortable. He started going to anatomy classes at the University of Southern California, studying the way the bones connect in the foot and which part of the foot holds the majority of a person's weight. With this knowledge, he began to make small changes in his shoe design so his clients would be not only fashionable but also comfortable. It was a brilliant move—his shoes became even more popular, and before long, he couldn't make shoes fast enough to keep up with all his customers' orders.

It was time to expand. But the American solution to the need to make more products at a faster rate was mass production, and Salvatore had already witnessed the kind of shoes that resulted in. He thought about hiring other shoemakers like himself to work in his shop, but he felt American shoemakers did not have the same focus on quality he had learned when he was a boy apprenticing in Italy. And so it was decided—Salvatore would move back to Italy, where he would open a shoe shop staffed with the best shoemakers he could find.

In 1927, Salvatore opened his shop in Florence, Italy. He designed the workshop carefully, combining assembly line techniques he'd learned in the Boston boot factory with the manual shoe-making techniques he'd been practicing for years. It worked wonderfully. Orders from American stars, as well as many other prominent people around the world, poured in.

But only two years later, the Great Depression left many Americans poor, and Salvatore's American sales dropped off. He continued to make shoes for Italians, though, and his business continued to expand. But then he faced another challenge: World War II was brewing, and the materials Salvatore used to make shoes, such as leather, were hard to find. But Salvatore had faced this kind of challenge before, back when he was nine and making shoes for his sister. He knew how to be creative while making shoes!

Some of Salvatore Ferragamo's most famous shoe designs are from this era. He designed women's shoes with cork soles that formed a wedge under the heel. Instead of using leather for the upper part of the shoe, he wove raffia to enclose the toe and wrap around the ankle. He also used hemp, plastic, wood, wire, felt, and fish skin as materials.

While World War II was taking over Europe and bombs were falling on Italy, Salvatore fell in love. In 1940 he married Wanda Miletti, from his hometown of Bonito, and they eventually had six children—three boys and three girls.

After World War II, Italy began rebuilding its country. People from all over the world started buying Salvatore's shoes again, and his success was seen as a symbol of Italy's bright future. In 1947 Salvatore won the prestigious Neiman Marcus Fashion Award for what he called invisible shoes. The straps were made of thin, clear plastic, but the wedge heel added height and shaped the person's feet and lower legs. It was a breakthrough in the fashion world, and the crowds went crazy for it.

Over the next few years, Salvatore would continue making shoes—one pair was crafted completely out of gold—while he also opened a store in New York City and started designing handbags. He died in 1960, but his wife and children continued the business for him.

Now, the Salvatore Ferragamo brand is famous for high-end shoes, bags, suits, scarves, ties, eyewear, watches, and perfume. Salvatore Ferragamo stores are open in cities around the world, including Shanghai, China, where a statue of a platform shoe adorns the front of the store. The Salvatore Ferragamo Museum in Italy opened in 1995 and was remodeled and expanded in 2006.

From his early shoe designs of cardboard and canvas to his fanciest shoes of pure gold, Salvatore Ferragamo's lifelong dedication to shoes has influenced fashion around the world. In 2003 Salvatore was honored as a fashion legend with the Rodeo Drive Walk of Style Award.

ROCK ON!

MICHAEL KEPLER MEO

Much like Yo-Yo Ma's mother, who heard a voice in her son's cello playing, Michael Kepler Meo's parents noticed something special about their son's voice, even when he was a toddler. By kindergarten, he was singing with the Portland Boychoir in Oregon, where he trained as a soprano. By ten, he was singing for the Portland Opera, and by eleven, the Houston Grand Opera. He tours around the country doing what he loves the most: singing professionally. Way to rock!

Jesse Owens

1913–1980 ◦ ATHLETE ◦ UNITED STATES

The minute you think you've got it beaten,
you're beaten. No matter what you did yesterday,
each sunrise wipes the slate clean.

—JESSE OWENS

Twelve-year-old Jesse Owens ran every race full out, as if he were running the 100-yard dash. That day in 1926, he was running the 220-yard dash against some of the best junior high runners in Cleveland. As usual, Jesse had pulled ahead of his competition at the start of the race. But, as was happening more and more often, runners inched by him on the track. When he finally reached the finish line, the tape was already fluttering in the breeze, broken by someone else. Today he came in third place. What was he doing wrong?

Jesse was so mad, he continued running at full speed until he plowed into the brick wall surrounding the track. Bouncing off, dazed and hurt, he looked up and saw Coach Riley looking down at him.

"Congratulations, Jesse! You won today. Even when the race was over, you didn't stop." Jesse thought his coach was making fun of him for running into the wall, but he was serious. Even though Jesse was still making the same mistakes he'd made the last year, his coach knew Jesse could be a champion. In that single display of fierceness, Coach Riley saw in Jesse the character and determination of an Olympian.

Back in 1926, this was a radical idea. Jesse was black and poor, and the Olympics were not exactly friendly to black athletes. Jesse's own dad, beaten down after a life of hard labor and discrimination, didn't want his son to get his hopes up for the Olympics. He told Jesse, "It don't do a colored man no good to get himself too high. 'Cause it's a [long] drop back to the bottom." But Coach Riley was right to dream big for Jesse, because ten years later, Jesse Owens stood in front of the world and accepted *four* Olympic gold medals in track.

Jesse Owens was born James Cleveland Owens in 1913 in Alabama to sharecropping parents. The life of a sharecropper was miserable—not much better than a slave's life. So, when the big cities of the North, like Detroit, Chicago, and Cleveland, began making cars and machines and hiring tons of workers, millions of blacks left the farms of the South, hoping to find a better life. Jesse's parents moved to Cleveland, Ohio, when Jesse (or J. C., as he was known then) was eight.

When he got to Cleveland, right from the start Jesse was at a disadvantage. Schools for blacks in the South were so bad that, by age nine, Jesse could barely read or write. He was put in the first grade, where he couldn't even fit into the tiny school desk. On his first day of school, when the teacher asked his name, he replied, "J. C., ma'am." Misunderstanding his Southern drawl, the teacher wrote down *Jesse*, and he was too intimidated to correct her.

His poor beginnings in school meant that he would struggle with his studies all the way through college. But there was one place where he excelled: on the track. "I always loved running," Jesse said. "It was something you could do . . . under your own power. You could go in any direction, fast or slow . . . fighting the wind . . . seeking out new sights just on the strength of your feet and the courage of your lungs."

In middle school, Jesse met the man who would change his life: Coach Riley. Because Jesse had to work after school to help support his family, he couldn't make it to regular track practices, so Coach Riley worked with Jesse early in the mornings before school started. He became Jesse's mentor, on and off the track.

For a while, Jesse lost most races, even though he was faster than anyone else. Before each race, he was doing the 1920s equivalent of trash-talking: staring his opponents down, trying to intimidate them before the race. Coach Riley watched in silence. It was only when Jesse asked, "Why can't I win?"

> Today's tracks, with their bouncy surface, give runners a lift and are made to drain water away so it doesn't form puddles. But in 1936 tracks were made from crushed cinders (pieces of partly burned coal). When it rained, the runners' heavy leather shoes soaked up the muck from the soggy track, slowing them down.

that day he crashed into the wall, that his coach did a peculiar thing. Instead of answering, he drove Jesse to a racetrack to watch horses run.

"What do you see on their faces?" Coach asked.

"Nothing," Jesse answered.

"That's right," Coach Riley noted. "Horses are honest. No animal has ever tried to stare another down . . . horses make it look easy because the determination is all on the inside where no one can see it."

From that day on, Jesse put his emotions aside when he ran, concentrated on his body—not his opponents—and tried to run like a horse, with an easy, fluid, and graceful power. He started winning!

At fifteen, he began setting world records for his age. He ran the 100-yard dash in eleven seconds. At eighteen, he became the high school world champion in the long jump; and at nineteen, he broke the world record for the 220-yard dash, at 20.7 seconds. Jesse, along with his teammate David Albritton, another future Olympian, helped their school earn first place in the most prestigious high school track meet in the Midwest. They came back to Cleveland as heroes. They were even welcomed by a parade. Jesse, now a nationally ranked athlete, was recruited by Ohio State University to run on its track team. Unlike today, when some college athletes are treated like campus royalty, attending school for free and living in luxury, in the 1930s, poor athletes had to work full-time to pay for their education. Jesse worked three jobs while going to class and competing.

Despite being one of Ohio State's biggest stars, Jesse was still discriminated against. Because he was black, he couldn't live on campus or eat in the restaurants near the school. When he and his teammates traveled to competitions, the whites rode in separate cars from the black athletes. In many gyms, the blacks weren't even allowed to take a shower. Jesse was frustrated that even though his white teammates were friendly, they did nothing to protest this racist treatment. As Jesse said, "Their niceness didn't include making sure you got to take your shower too." But those hard times helped strengthen Jesse's character and prepared him for the difficult challenges to come.

> Jesse was finally honored by the United States president for his accomplishments at the 1936 Olympics—in 1976! President Gerald Ford awarded him the Medal of Freedom, the highest honor our country can pay to a civilian in peacetime.

After an incredible season in 1935 where, in one day, Jesse smashed three world records and tied a fourth, he began thinking he might actually make it to the 1936 Olympics. Sure enough, a few months later he was chosen for the US Olympic track team and hopped a ship to Europe for the Olympics. That year, they were being held in Nazi-controlled Berlin. The Nazis hated Jews, blacks, and other groups that they called nonhumans. The pressure was on the German athletes to show that

Hitler was right when he claimed that the Aryans (white, blue-eyed, blond-haired people) were the "master race." And just as much pressure was on the United States, with its ten black athletes, to show how wrong Hitler was.

Jesse felt the pressures of competition, race, and his incredible fame at the Olympics. He awoke one morning to a hoard of autograph seekers thrusting their arms through his open hotel window. But he remembered Coach Riley's lesson. He kept his emotions in control, and he won four gold medals for the United States in the 100-meter dash, the long jump, the 200-meter run, and the 400-meter relay. He also won the hearts of the German fans with his grace, sportsmanship, and awesome speed. And, just as he'd learned to do at home, he ignored Hitler's racism. He even became friends, much to Hitler's anger, with Germany's top track star, Luz Long. The world loved Jesse, not just for his running, but for his ability to keep his cool under tough circumstances.

> In Berlin, the street outside the Olympic Stadium has been renamed Jesse Owens Strasse (street).
>
> ⁓

Despite his star status, life wasn't easy when Jesse got home. As a black man in America, most doors were closed to him. When he couldn't find a job to support his wife and family, he was forced to humiliate himself by racing against horses for pay. His first real job was as a playground instructor earning thirty dollars a week—not a lot of money even then. But over the years, as America's racism eased and Jesse's achievements were recognized, life got better. He counseled young people, taught sports clinics for the government during World War II, and started his own public relations agency. In the 1970s he became an activist for racial equality, fighting for equal housing laws for blacks, and as an adviser to baseball's American League, pushing team owners to hire black managers.

Despite Jesse's struggles against racism, he lived his life with dignity, never returning hatred with hatred, and always trying to change people's minds by his own fairness and honesty. He said:

No matter how much bad there is, the best way to get rid of it is by exposing the good. *Don't just hack away at the roots of evil. They go all the way to China. Plant next to prejudice another tree that grows so big and high that discrimination has to wither and die.*[6]

HOW WILL YOU ROCK THE WORLD?

I am going to rock the world by becoming a famous athlete. To be precise, an NHL hockey star. I started skating lessons and hockey initiation when I was five and started real lessons when I was eight. I am now eleven and in the squirt level in hockey. I've got a long way to go to get to the NHL. I'm going to try hard to accomplish my dream to rock this world.

MYLES SCHMERTZLER · AGE 11

Nelson Mandela

1918– ⚬ ACTIVIST ⚬ SOUTH AFRICA

The struggle is my life. I will continue fighting for freedom until the end of my days.

—NELSON MANDELA

The crowd hushed as the chief began speaking: "We are here today to celebrate our sons becoming men." Rolihlahla glanced at the other teenage boys. Like him, they were painted from head to toe in white earth to symbolize their purity for this coming-of-age ceremony. For weeks they'd been living in grass huts apart from their families. Now their whole village was here to celebrate their return as men. He couldn't wait to see what gifts he would get. Some sheep? Maybe even a cow or two of his own?

He snapped back to attention as the chief's voice turned angry. "We promise them manhood, but it's a promise we can't fulfill. For we Xhosas, and all black South Africans, are a conquered people." He pointed at the boys: "Here are chiefs who will never rule because we have no power to govern ourselves; scholars who will never teach because we have no place for them to study." He looked at the proud families and finished sadly, "These gifts we bring them today are nothing, for we cannot give them the greatest gift of all: freedom and independence."

Rolihlahla thought about the chief's words as he ceremonially burned the grass hut filled with his boyhood belongings. His uncle, his mother, his whole village expected him to become a chief. But he was beginning to see there were some things more important than becoming a chief. He wanted to help his people fight for equality with the white man. That day he realized he would have to leave his village and his family's wishes behind. In fact, he would have to leave his entire childhood behind. As he watched the flames devour the hut, Rolihlahla shivered; not from the cold, but from his own fear of the future.

Rolihlahla had good reason to be afraid. Ever since whites had landed in South Africa hundreds of years before, they had stolen land from black Africans and prevented them from having any power in the government. There were five times as many black people as whites, yet blacks were allowed to keep only 13 percent of the land in the country—and only the very worst land. Rolihlahla would grow up and risk his life fighting these injustices. He would become known as Nelson Mandela, the most famous prisoner in the world, and he would sacrifice his own freedom to lead his people and his country into a new future.

As a child, Nelson loved to herd cattle and hunt birds with a slingshot. He was also excellent at stick-fighting, a traditional African sport.

Nelson was born in 1918 in a small village, and his father was a chief of the Thembu people, who are part of the larger Xhosa tribe. At birth he was named Rolihlahla, which means "troublemaker." Little did his parents know how much trouble their son would make one day! When Rolihlahla started school, a white teacher couldn't pronounce his name. "From now on, your name is Nelson," she told him. The name stuck.

His father had hoped Nelson would become a chief, but he died when his son was just nine. Nelson's mother knew it would be difficult getting an education for her son without her husband's help, so she sent Nelson away to be raised by a family friend, Jongintaba, the head chief of all the Thembu people. Nelson was sad to leave, but he was quickly accepted as a part of Jongintaba's family and was treated just like a son in the royal household.

Nelson's passion for justice was born as he watched the chief settle tribal disputes. While the white government made laws without giving black people any say, Thembu chiefs listened to all members of the tribe, and a decision was made only if everyone could agree. Nelson wanted to bring that kind of justice to all South African blacks, not just his own tribe, so he decided to become a lawyer instead of a chief.

After his coming-of-age ceremony, Nelson left his village to attend an all-black university. When he and other students protested the school's white administration, the principal asked them to stop—and most students gave in. Nelson wouldn't back down, however, and he got kicked out. He knew Jongintaba would be furious, so he ran away to the big city: Johannesburg.

Johannesburg, which was built around diamond mines, attracted thousands of black people from the countryside who were looking for work. Blacks weren't allowed to live near whites, so they had to live in areas outside the city called townships, crowded together in tiny, tin-roofed shacks with dirt floors, no running water, no heat, and no

> Nelson was so poor when he arrived in Johannesburg that he often walked the 12 miles round-trip to work just to save on bus fare.

electricity. Nelson was shocked by the poverty and the racism that caused it, but he was also excited about the political activity going on around him. Other black Africans were fighting back. They had created the African National Congress (ANC) to demand their human rights and equality. Nelson signed up and soon became one of the ANC's leaders.

And just in time. In 1948, the white government turned the unofficial rules separating blacks and whites into formal law, called apartheid. *Apartheid* means "apartness," and the new laws kept the races separated. Whites had total control. *Whites Only* signs went up everywhere, forbidding blacks to use buses, restaurants, beaches—basically everything. Blacks had to carry identification with them at all times. They were told where to live, work, and go to school. They were forbidden to marry anyone outside their race. If they broke an apartheid law, they went to jail.

Nelson planned protests, boycotts of white-owned businesses, and mass strikes, which thousands of blacks took part in. By refusing to work, shop, ride buses, or go to school, black Africans peacefully shut the city down. While he was protesting, Nelson was also busy getting his law degree. In 1952, he and a friend, Oliver Tambo, opened Johannesburg's first black law firm: Mandela & Tambo. They were immediately swamped with clients. Nelson describes a typical morning:

We had to move through a crowd of people in the hallways, on the stairs, and in our small waiting room. Africans were desperate for legal help . . . it was a crime to walk through a Whites Only door, a crime to ride a Whites Only bus . . . a crime to be unemployed and a crime to be employed in the wrong place, a crime to live in certain places and a crime to have no place to live.[7]

During the 1950s, black Africans lost more and more rights every day. In 1960 the fight against apartheid turned violent when five thousand blacks gathered to protest in a township called Sharpeville. Even though the protesters were peaceful, white police opened fire on them and mowed down sixty-nine innocent people—most of them shot in the back as they were trying to run away. The rest of the world was horrified by the violence. But instead of loosening the apartheid rules, the government cracked down harder. Now blacks couldn't be on the streets after sundown and couldn't gather in public at all. The ANC was outlawed.

After the Sharpeville Massacre, Nelson felt that it was time to try other methods. Many blacks were getting killed during peaceful protests. He decided it was time to fight back. As an ANC leader, he urged the use of force against *symbols* of apartheid—government buildings, railroads, factories—but not against *people*. When bombs started going off, it didn't take long for the police to figure out who was behind them. In 1963, Nelson and other ANC leaders were arrested and put to trial.

People around the world awaited the verdict. Nearly everyone was sure the ANC leaders would get the death penalty. Nelson wasn't afraid, however, and he said to the court:

> *During my lifetime I have dedicated myself to the struggle of the African people. . . . I have cherished the ideal of a democratic and free society. . . . It is an ideal which I hope to live for and achieve. But, if needs be, it is an ideal for which I am prepared to die.*[8]

To everyone's surprise, Nelson and the others were not sentenced to death, but instead, to spend the rest of their lives in prison on Robben Island.

Robben Island Prison was a lot like the prison at Alcatraz Island in California—prisoners could see the mainland, but escape was impossible: the freezing water surrounding the island was filled with sharks! Nelson refused to lose his fighting spirit. In his first day in prison, a guard ordered him to jog. He refused. When the guard

When the ANC was banned, Mandela had to go into hiding for a year. He hid in empty houses and wore disguises whenever he went out. He was so hard to catch, the press dubbed him the Black Pimpernel after a famous British play about a spy, THE SCARLET PIMPERNEL. Once, when disguised as a chauffeur, Nelson drove up right next to the chief of police! The disguise fooled him, and Nelson escaped again.

threatened Nelson, he growled back, "If you so much as lay a hand on me, I will take you to the highest court in the land, and when I finish with you, you will be as poor as a church mouse." The guard never bothered him again.

Although the prisoners spent their days crushing stones into gravel or digging pits, Nelson kept their minds sharp. He successfully demanded that the prison create a library. Each day, while they worked, the prisoners taught each other all they'd learned about history, politics, philosophy, and economics. Many of them finished high school and college while in jail. Soon the prison was nicknamed "Mandela University."

As life in South Africa continued to get worse for black Africans in the 1970s and '80s, and as their clashes with whites grew increasingly violent, the name Nelson Mandela spread around the world, drawing attention to the horrors of apartheid. A song called "Free Nelson Mandela" was a huge hit. Daily protests in American and European cities pressured governments to boycott South Africa—people stopped buying their diamonds, companies pulled out of the country, and foreign banks stopped loaning money to the government.

Isolated from the rest of the world, its economy in shambles from boycotts, the South African government had no choice. It offered to free Nelson if he promised to stop the violence. But the government still wasn't promising to end apartheid, so Nelson rejected the offer. After more than twenty years in jail, he refused to leave until apartheid was gone and *all* black Africans were free. In 1989, as the world grew more and more disgusted with South Africa, a new president, F. W. de Klerk, was elected—he immediately began secret negotiations with Nelson.

In prison, communication between the political prisoners was often forbidden. They got around this rule by writing and passing secret notes on toilet paper.

De Klerk surprised the world on February 11, 1990, when he suddenly announced the end of apartheid and set Nelson Mandela free after twenty-seven years in prison. Together they began the difficult process of creating a new, democratic South Africa for all people, regardless of their skin color. In 1993 they were jointly awarded the world's highest honor, the Nobel Peace Prize, for working to end apartheid. A year later, for the first time in South Africa's history, blacks and whites voted together in democratic elections. After a lifetime of fighting for freedom and equality, Nelson was elected president of South Africa.

It was no easy job. He somehow had to bring blacks and whites together. He refused to take revenge on whites, and instead focused on creating a new future together while improving housing, education, and employment for black Africans. At the 1995 Rugby World Cup, tens of thousands of white fans cheered "Nelson, Nelson" as their president walked onto the field in a team jersey. A fellow political prisoner explains the importance of the appearance, "The liberation struggle ... was about liberating white people from fear. And there it was ... fear melting away." Nelson understood that it would take both blacks *and* whites to repair the broken country.

> The 2009 movie INVICTUS, starring Matt Damon and directed by Clint Eastwood, tells the story of Nelson Mandela's passion for rugby and how he used it to connect with South Africans of all races.

After centuries of inequality, life in South Africa is still not perfect. But the changes that have taken place since the end of apartheid are amazing. Blacks can live, work, and study wherever they want. They are free to follow their dreams. The *Whites Only* signs are gone. And it was Nelson Mandela who sacrificed most of his life to see those changes happen. He is a symbol of the dreams and struggles of oppressed people everywhere. His is the boy who could have been chief of his village but who instead became a hero for the world.

ROCK ON!

GREGORY R. SMITH

When was the last time you heard about a nine-year-old graduating from high school? It doesn't happen every day! Greg Smith earned his bachelor's degree from Randolph-Macon College as a preteen, and then on his fourteenth birthday, he started graduate school at the University of Virginia. But perhaps even more impressive is Greg's dedication to advocating for children's rights. He travels around the world—whenever he's not in class—to talk about the importance of education for all children. He has spearheaded humanitarian movements for children in Brazil, Rwanda, and Kenya. For all of his work, Greg has been nominated for a Nobel Peace Prize four times.

StaN Lee

1922– ☀ WRITER AND ILLUSTRATOR ☀ UNITED STATES

No single figure can lay claim to the omnipresent
influence that Lee has had on American comic
books and on popular culture.

—JEFF MCLAUGHLIN, EDITOR

Stanley ran to the mailbox and threw open the flap. Inside were three envelopes, and he sifted through them until he saw what he was looking for: a letter from the *Herald-Tribune*. The newspaper had an ongoing contest called The Biggest News of the Week, and Stanley had won the past two weeks in a row. He hoped he won again.

He ripped open the envelope and pulled out the page inside. Yes, he had won again! But there was more to the letter. Stan read on and found that the editor of the *Herald-Tribune* was politely asking him not to enter the contest again. Stanley's writing was so good, the editor wrote, that nobody else had a chance. He ended the letter with a recommendation that Stanley think about writing professionally. At just fifteen years old, the news editor at one of the most important papers in New York was telling him he wrote like a professional!

Stanley Lee was born Stanley Lieber in his parents' New York City apartment in 1922. His mom and dad had emigrated from Romania, and Stanley was their first son. The family did not have much money, though, and when Stanley's little brother, Larry, was born, they had even less. Stanley remembered his parents always fighting about money. His father would leave every day to look for work, but every night when he came home and still didn't have a job, the family's future looked even bleaker. Every few years, they moved when they could no longer afford the apartment they were staying in. To keep from getting too depressed about all this, Stanley read—a lot. In the living room, at school, at the dining room table, everywhere. He loved the Hardy Boys series, and if he didn't have a good book, he'd read the food labels on the boxes and bottles on the table in front of him.

> Stanley has always preferred to read while eating. When he was a kid, his mom bought him a stand for holding his books, complete with clips at the bottom to hold the pages open, because he was always reading at the table.

Stanley was good at school too. He was always breezing through his homework, and his mom wanted him to finish school early so he could work and help support the family, so he skipped some grades. Being the youngest kid in class by a couple years meant Stanley didn't have a lot of friends, though, so he continued to read as an escape. And he started to draw.

In the fantastical world in Stanley's mind, people wearing capes were flying in the sky, and that's just what he drew—starting with one line across the page to separate the ground from the sky and then a few stick figures up with the clouds. Then he began adding words and boxes, connecting more pictures to the first one, so when they all lined up, they told a story.

In high school, Stanley started writing for money, but it wasn't as glamorous as he'd hoped. He was an obituary writer, and it was so depressing always writing about dead people. Then he started writing for the National Tuberculosis Hospital. Again, though, Stanley thought the writing was boring and dreary. He tried some nonwriting jobs for a while until his Uncle Robbie told him the publishing company he worked for might need some help. Now that Stanley was finished with high school, he should talk to the hiring manager.

That publishing company was Timely Comics, now known as Marvel Comics. When Stanley was hired on as an assistant in 1939, at just seventeen years old, he had no idea he was launching his lifelong career.

Timely Comics published—you guessed it—comic books. It was owned by Martin Goodman, who was Stanley's uncle, but they didn't know each other very well yet. Over the years, Stanley would learn a lot about comics and business from his uncle. One of Timely's biggest superheroes in 1939 was Captain America, created by Joe Simon and Jack Kirby, two of the comics world's most influential writers and artists. One of Stanley's first assignments was to write two pages of filler text to go into the latest *Captain America* issue. He titled it "Captain America Foils the Traitor's Revenge" and signed it Stan Lee. He didn't want to use his real name because he thought he might write serious novels in the future. *A pen name would be better for this silly comic book stuff,* he thought. Years later, when he no longer thought writing for comics was silly, Stanley Lieber would permanently change his name to Stan Lee.

Stan was afraid to go to war, but he thought enlisting in the Army was the right thing to do when so many other young men were fighting. He never ended up fighting, though, because the Army found out he was a writer and assigned him to write manuals.

In 1941 Joe and Jack decided to leave Timely Comics. Because there was no one else in the comics department, and because Stan had already helped with about a dozen comic book issues, Mr. Goodwin told Stan he could make the comics until they were able to find someone more experienced. But Mr. Goodwin never hired anybody else. At eighteen years old, Stan was in charge of what Timely Comics published!

With the exception of 1942 to 1945, when Stan served in the Army for World War II, Stan remained editor in chief at Timely Comics until 1972, when he was promoted to publisher. The 1950s proved to be tough for the comics world, though. People started blaming children's poor behavior and dirty language on comic books, and sales dropped. But then Julius Schwartz from DC Comics came up with the Justice League of America, and comics readers went wild again. Mr. Goodwin tasked Stan with creating a similar team of superheroes.

Stan talked with Jack Kirby about this assignment, and they agreed it was a good idea to create superheroes who had human problems with things like love, money, greed, and family—issues their powers couldn't fix for them. By the early 1960s, Timely was renamed to Marvel Comics, and Jack came back to the company to help Stan. Together they created the Fantastic Four, with the human flaws they had agreed upon. It was a stroke of genius! Teen readers loved that they could relate to the heroes' problems while still looking up to them.

Stan and Jack reveled in this new popularity and kept going. Soon they had also created the X-Men, Iron Man, the Incredible Hulk, and the Silver Surfer. The duo's most successful character of all time was Spider-Man.

And Stan changed the face of comic book production. Instead of just crediting the writer and penciller for each comic, he also acknowledged the inker and letterer. When he was very busy, Stan would have brainstorm sessions with the artists and then write a basic summary of what would happen in the comic issue. From that, the artists would draw all the panels and give the work back to Stan, who would write in the words. This method gave artists more control over the creative process, and it freed up Stan's time so he could work on more comics.

Stan also developed three Spider-Man issues that depicted drug use. This was considered unacceptable in the comics world, even though the context of the story was that drugs could do a lot of harm. Marvel Comics published them anyway, and they sold incredibly well. This inspired other comic makers to push the boundaries for the sake of helping kids learn. Stan especially wanted kids to learn not to be prejudiced.

The 1980s saw lots of comics turned into movies and television cartoon series, and Stan moved to California to help. Since then, the trend has hardly slowed. *Iron Man* and *The X-Men* are two popular series, not to mention *The Fantastic Four* and *Spider-Man*. And he's helped with the video games too! Stan narrated the three Spider-Man games that came out in 2000, 2001, and 2010. Despite his work on the television and movie series, Stan still writes and edits Marvel comic books as he has done for more than seventy years. He's even helped DC Comics with a couple of their products over the years.

Every Marvel comic book featured "Stan's Soapbox," where Stan wrote about upcoming projects from Marvel and also about current events. In the 1950s and 1960s, civil rights were a hot topic in America, and Stan spoke out against racism.

In 1994 Stan won the Will Eisner Comics Industry Award and was inducted into the Hall of Fame. His autobiography, *Excelsior!*, was published in 2002, and in 2010 the History Channel released a documentary called *Stan Lee's Superhumans*.

HOW WILL YOU ROCK THE WORLD?

My dream is to become an illustrator of books. I love to draw and create images that come alive on paper. This will rock the world because I will turn words into pictures and become a famous illustrator. I want to create a whole new technique for illustrating that explains things as well as words can. This will help people visualize their world in a whole new way.

DANIEL SOLOW ⚛ AGE 11

Vidal Sassoon

1928–2012 ❈ HAIR STYLIST ❈ ENGLAND AND UNITED STATES

Swinging London—which dominated many facets of popular culture in the 1960s with Beatlemania, miniskirts, bell-bottoms, etc.—was the scene of one of the truly revolutionary developments in modern hair styling, the Vidal Sassoon haircut.

—FRANK W. HOFFMAN, PHD, AND WILLIAM G. BAILEY, MA, FASHION WRITERS

L isten carefully, Vidal." The teenage boy's mother shook him awake. Then she told him all about the dream she'd just had—how she'd seen an older version of him working in a barber shop and making enough money never to have to live in poverty again.

"Mum, that's ridiculous," Vidal protested. At fourteen, he didn't want to cut or style hair. It was 1942, and World War II was raging throughout Europe. Vidal Sassoon wanted to be a politician so he could fight against Fascism and Nazism for the safety and fair treatment of Jews and other minorities. He was Jewish, and it was terrifying to watch how brutally the Jews were being treated across the continent. But his mother told him not to argue. She signed him up to apprentice with Adolph Cohen, the hairdresser in the East End of London.

Vidal Sassoon was born in 1928 in West London, England, to a Jewish mother from Spain. Over the course of his life, Vidal became incredibly close to his mother, but his youth was fraught with hardship. His father left the family when Vidal was only three, and his mother could no longer afford to pay rent on the small apartment she lived in with Vidal and her youngest son, Ivor. She packed up and moved the boys with her to live with her sister. Between the two families, seven people shared the small apartment, and they were constantly struggling for money. After two years with five growing children, they just couldn't all fit in the same rooms anymore. But Vidal's mother still didn't have enough money to rent her own apartment for her family. She turned to the church, specifically the church orphanage, to help her.

At five years old, Vidal went to live at the Spanish and Portuguese Jewish Orphanage. Ivor followed shortly after. The first night in the orphanage, Vidal curled up into a ball on his bed, and all the other boys left him alone. They knew the sadness he felt because they had felt it too. Vidal and Ivor lived in the orphanage for almost seven years. They made friends there, but they were hungry most of the time, and their mother was only allowed to visit once a month. More than anything, Vidal longed to live with his family again.

Then one day his wish came true. His mother had remarried, and the family now had enough money for Vidal and Ivor to move home. That's when his mom had the dream that would shape Vidal's future.

At Cohen's salon, Vidal learned how to cut and style hair. He mostly worked with women, and the common practice of the time was for ladies to come to the salon once a week to have their hair curled and styled, then dried under the hair-drying hoods, and sprayed with so much hair spray, it would barely move until their appointment the following week. And the salons were stuffy. Stylists were expected to be silent so the customers could relax while they quietly read their magazines and waited for their hair to be done. Vidal did what he had to in order to make his boss and customers happy, but he was not excited about the work.

After the war, Vidal joined the 43 Group. These boys went out every night and fought with the Blackshirts, a fascist gang in London. Even though Fascism and the racism it preached were technically defeated in World War II, many people still supported it and acted on it. Vidal believed such discrimination was wrong, so he resisted it. He'd often come to work with black eyes or other minor injuries from his skirmishes the night before, and he'd have to come up with a vague excuse, like slipping on a hair pin, to explain.

Then in 1947 the United Nations voted for Israel to be its own state, a safe place for Jews. Vidal went to Israel as a volunteer to help defend it from attackers. But when his mother sent a telegram that his stepfather had suffered a heart attack and Vidal was needed at home, he left the cause in others' hands.

> Vidal was drafted into the British army, but he went AWOL after an officer insulted his Jewish heritage. A firm believer in racial equality, Vidal considered leaving the army a protest.

Vidal never stopped supporting the fight for equality and the Jews' right to inhabit Israel, but when he returned to London, his career really began. For a long time, he'd wanted to break out of the poor neighborhoods of London, but he knew that if he went to a wealthier part of the city, his accent would give him away. To overcome that, he'd been going to the theater and practicing what he called a posh accent for years, and he thought he finally had it down. He set up a salon on Bond Street and hoped to fit in with his new neighbors. It worked! Everybody loved him, and they let him experiment on their hair with new cuts and styles.

By the sixties, Vidal Sassoon was known for his practical approach to hairstyling. He knew women didn't *really* want to come to the salon every week and then spend the next seven days with a stiff 'do. So he cut their hair so it could relax—and not be varnished with chemicals—to look good. And he was just in time too. Those were the days of The Beatles and bell-bottoms. Nobody wanted their mother's hairdo!

That's exactly the reason why fashion designer Mary Quant went to Vidal in 1963 when she needed new haircuts for all of her models for an upcoming fashion show. The new clothing design featured high collars, and the models' long hair covered them up. But they definitely didn't want the typical short hair styles like everyone else was doing. They wanted something new, trendy, and fun.

Vidal fulfilled the order perfectly. He came up with asymmetrical cuts, with the hair chin-length on one side and shorter on the other, and the five-point cut, which formed two points in front of the ears and three more points at the nape of the neck. The fashion world loved Vidal's creations, and soon he was dubbed the founder of modern hairdressing.

> Vidal gave his haircuts names, just like an artist names his sculptures. Some of his most famous designs were called Eye-Eye and the Curly Geometric.
>
> —m—

Women all over England, the rest of Europe, and even America began wearing their hair in Vidal's styles. With that, Vidal soon set up more salons in England and then expanded to America. And he redefined salons from being quiet and stuffy, like where he had apprenticed, to being loud, social, and fun. He played rock music, and his stylists wore trendy clothes, flinging their blow dryers from their belts as if they were gunslingers in the Wild West. It seemed everyone in the world wanted to go to a Vidal Sassoon salon.

Today, Vidal Sassoon Hair Academies teach aspiring hair stylists in London and Santa Monica, California. Sassoon salons can be found all over the United Kingdom, America, Canada, and Germany, and a whole line of hair care products features Vidal's name. Vidal retired in 2004, but he devoted much of his time to supporting racial equality. In 1982 he started the Vidal Sassoon International Center for the Study of Antisemitism at Hebrew University in Israel, where students study the phenomenon of racism against Jews and how it affects the world. He lived in Los Angeles and devoted his time and money to similar causes until his death in 2012.

ROCK ON!

KIERON WILLIAMSON

Kieron Williamson doesn't paint your typical pictures to hang on the refrigerator door. At nine years old, he paints scenes and portraits that are exhibited all over the world. Kieron started painting as a five-year-old when his family was on vacation in Cornwall, England. The boats in the nearby port served as inspiration for what would prove to be Kieron's amazing talent. After a few art classes, Kieron and his art made their first public appearance when Kieron was six, and the exhibit sold out in fourteen minutes! Now Kieron paints every day but also enjoys going to school and playing soccer.

Mau Piailug

1932–2010 ⊚ EXPLORER ⊚ MICRONESIA

If you can read the ocean, if you can see the island in your mind, you will never get lost.

—MAU PIAILUG

au wanted to cheer when the master of the induction ceremony smeared the medicinal herbs on his forehead and chest. It symbolized that he had the right mind and heart to be a *palu*, or traditional sea navigator who uses only natural elements to guide his way. To the people of Satawal, a small island in the Pacific Ocean, a *palu* is even more important than a chief!

When the ceremony master was finished, the people of his island threw garlands around his neck and sprinkled turmeric—a symbol of knowledge—over him. Everyone feasted on fish, turtle, and breadfruit. Mau felt like a hero.

Mau was born in 1932 on the island of Satawal in Micronesia. His real name was Pius Piailug, but he earned the nickname Mau with his boating habits. *Maumau* means "strong," and Mau was definitely strong. As far back as he could remember, his Grandfather Raangipi would set him in tide pools in the ocean so Mau could feel the way the water moved around the sand and rocks, surging in toward the land and then rushing back out to sea. Once Mau had grown a bit, Raangipi began taking him on his large canoe out to the deep sea.

But when Mau got seasick, it looked like the fate his grandfather had chosen for him wouldn't work at all. He felt his stomach flip and his throat burn, and he gripped the handrail as hard as he could to try to keep from throwing up. Raangipi knew just the trick, though. He tied young Mau to the back of the canoe, dragging Mau's body through the water while ocean spray occasionally splashed his face. Believe it or not, it worked! Mau never got seasick again.

The next step was to start memorizing the stars. Grandpa Raangipi made a classroom on the beach, using pebbles of worn-down coral and laying them out in the sand in the shapes of star constellations. Then he added a palm frond to represent the boat. Mau learned how the stars move from east to west every night and how their locations change throughout the year. He also learned that the waves change when land is nearby, just as the types of birds one sees and how those birds act can mean a boat is nearing an island. If Mau paid close attention to these details, his grandfather instructed him, he would never get lost, and he would always find his destination—no matter how small the island was.

Mau was just thirteen when his grandfather died, but he continued to study navigation with his father for the next five years. When he was eighteen, his island community honored him as the newest *palu*, and he could

> A navigator can learn a lot about his location from the birds and the fish. Sweeter tasting fish mean a river is nearby, which means land is too. Some kinds of birds dive to catch their own fish far out at sea, spending days flying and floating on the water, but other kinds live on land and only go out to sea to hunt for a day at a time. When those birds are near, so is an island.

not have been more proud of his work and everything his grandfather had taught him.

Satawal island is only about a mile long and a half mile wide, and the closest island is 140 miles away. Deliveries of food, clothes, and other goods have to be brought by ship. Nowadays, the ship comes once a month, but when Mau was a kid, it only came once every three months. The island people had to know how to deep-sea fish, because it could be a long time before they received another shipment of food.

Mau fished often, but with the navigation skills that his grandfather and father had taught him, he could also boat to Palau, Guam, and other islands if he needed to pick up something that was too important to wait for the next ship. Without the use of any compass or map, Mau always reached his destination.

In 1973, Mau visited his niece and her husband, Mike McCoy, in Hawaii. When Mike invited Mau to attend a meeting of the Polynesian Voyaging Society, he was intrigued and went along. The people at the meeting were trying to determine if ancient seafarers could have traveled some of the great distances that today's ships travel. They were especially interested in the 2,400-mile trek between Hawaii and Tahiti. Stories had been passed down through the generations of brave and intelligent men who went to sea for a month or more to travel the distance. Modern sailors, however, argued that it would be impossible to accurately navigate to such small islands without the use of a compass. If the navigator was off by even a fraction of a degree, he could miss his destination island completely.

HOKULE'A means "Star of Gladness," referring to Arcturus, one of the brightest stars in the northern hemisphere's sky.

There was only one way to find out who was right: try it. Then Mau realized why Mike had invited him to the meeting. The Polynesian Voyaging Society already had a boat—a double-hulled canoe called *Hokule'a* built in the Hawaiian traditional style—but they didn't know anybody who had experience navigating without a compass or a map. It was not just that Mau was perfect for the job, he was the *only* person at that time who had the know-how to complete the mission. All the

Hawaiian *palus* had grown old and died without younger navigators to take their place.

In the spring of 1976, Mau and a crew of fifteen people set out for Tahiti in the *Hokule'a*. He took gourds filled with water and root vegetables tied up in leaves. Under the starry sky, he located the star that would lead them to their destination. He paid attention to the way the winds gusted and the colors the seawater reflected onto the clouds above. Every last detail of the environment was a clue to Mau, and he watched them all carefully to make sure they stayed on course. One month later Mau spotted a group of white terns flying overhead. He knew they were close to Mataiva Atoll, the island next to Tahiti, and their journey was almost over.

On the thirty-second day, Tahiti was in sight, and as Mau directed the boat to port, the crew was astonished to see a crowd of 1,600 people cheering for them! The successful completion of the journey meant several things. First, it proved that the stories the elders told of their ancestors crossing the sea from island to island were true. Second, it meant that the ancestors of the native peoples of the South Pacific islands—Micronesia, Polynesia, Hawaii, and others—had intentionally migrated to other islands and spread their culture. Third, it symbolized the lifting of colonial power in Tahiti—European colonists had settled the islands as early as the 1700s, and by the 1900s, many aspects of the natives' traditions were forbidden. Now the people rejoiced in the modern reenactment of their ancestors' practices, and interest in traditional navigation surged.

By this time, Mau was in his forties, and he knew it was time to start teaching younger people the skills his grandfather had taught him. He'd tried to apprentice some of the boys on Satawal, but they were not interested in Mau's ancient practice. Traditionally, Mau's culture forbade him from sharing the secrets of the *palu* with people of other cultures, but he knew that rule was outdated. If he waited for the boys of Satawal to show interest, he could be waiting forever! When he witnessed the avid interest displayed by Hawaiians, Tahitians, and others, Mau knew he had found his students.

Over the next thirty years, Mau spent his time teaching and leading more voyages. In 2000 the Smithsonian Institute and the National

Museum of Natural History honored Mau's dedication to traditional navigation and his role in spreading interest and knowledge of this ancient technique. He also received the Robert J. Pfeiffer Medal from the Bishop Museum in 2008. Perhaps the most important honor Mau received was from the Hawaiian people in 2007, though. The Polynesian Voyaging Society in Hawaii presented Mau with a handcrafted boat called *Alingano Maisu* as a token of their appreciation for Mau's dedication to passing on his knowledge.

Mau died in 2010. People around the world acknowledged the passing of this incredible man. Following Micronesian tradition, Mau's family closed the seas in the area for nine days to honor the *palu's* death.

ROCK ON!

JORDAN ROMERO

When thirteen-year-old Jordan Romero takes a trip with his family, it involves climbing a mountain. Since 2006, Team Jordan—consisting of Jordan and his dad and stepmom, Paul Romero and Karen Lundgren, as well as others along the way—has been scaling the highest peaks on every continent, also known as the Seven Summits. They reached the summit of Mount Vinson in Antarctica in December 2011, the last in the series. Jordan has already started his next project. On the B.I.G. Tour, Jordan travels to each of the fifty states to meet kids and talk about staying healthy. Then he climbs the state's highest peak. You can come too!

The Dalai Lama

1935– ◈ SPIRITUAL AND POLITICAL LEADER ◈ TIBET AND INDIA

*For as long as space endures, and for as long as living beings remain,
until then may I, too . . . dispel the misery of the world.*

—THE DALAI LAMA

The mud hut was dark and cold, with only a yak-oil lamp lighting the room. The traveling merchants couldn't believe that this shabby house in such a remote village might be the right one, but they carefully laid out dozens of objects just in case.

"Show us the things that belong to you," whispered the oldest merchant to the small boy. The boy's parents were bewildered as their son picked up a drum and then some old prayer beads. "It's mine. It's mine," he said confidently each time. The merchants raised their eyebrows at each other—the items had belonged to their dead leader. The boy chose correctly. *Perhaps we have found him after all*, they secretly hoped.

Their hearts sank, however, when the boy struggled over his final choice. He stared at two nearly identical walking sticks but couldn't choose between them. Everyone in the room held their breath. Were the earlier choices just a coincidence? As they began to give up hope, the boy smiled and took hold of the correct cane. The adults let out a collective sigh of relief.

"The prophecies were correct," the old merchant cried joyfully. "We have found our Dalai Lama!" The boy's parents gasped in surprise as the merchants removed their disguises. The "merchants" were really high officials from the holy city of Lhasa, and after years of searching, they had finally found the next god-king of Tibet.

The young Dalai Lama was very mechanical. He could fix clocks and watches like a pro. He rebuilt an old car and raced it around the palace courtyard (there were no roads in Tibet!), and even started his own movie theater with a broken-down projector and some old newsreels.

Tibet, located high in the Himalayan Mountains between China and India, is a Buddhist country. Followers of the Buddhist religion believe in reincarnation: when a person dies, his or her soul is reborn into another living form. You could come back as a person, an animal, or even a bug! They also believe that their leader, the Dalai Lama, is always the reincarnation of the original Dalai Lama, who ruled Tibet in the 1300s. When a Dalai Lama dies, they must find the new child his soul has been reborn into.

When the thirteenth Dalai Lama died, officials scoured the land looking for his reincarnation. Meanwhile, in a small village in northeast Tibet, the future Dalai Lama, Lhamo Dhondrub, was born in 1935. Although he was raised as a normal boy, he was always different. As soon as he could talk, the unusual boy told everyone that his home was really in Lhasa and demanded to sit at the head of the table, instead of his father!

Before being discovered as the Dalai Lama, one of Lhamo's favorite pastimes was hanging out in the chicken coop, pretending to be a chicken. He even sat on the nests!

As a boy, the Dalai Lama was a bit of a troublemaker, but the monks couldn't punish him. How could they spank their holy ruler? When he got into trouble, they spanked his brother instead, hoping this would make him feel guilty enough to stop!

━ᘛ━

Back in Lhasa, the monks' search for their reincarnated leader was guided by a vision. Looking into the waters of a sacred pool, they saw a temple with a blue roof and a house with strange wooden rain gutters. After years of searching, they finally found the temple and the house—it was the home of two-year-old Lhamo.

After testing the boy with the belongings of the previous Dalai Lama, the monks took their new leader and his family to the city of Lhasa where he moved into the Potala Palace. While *you* might be psyched to move into a palace with a thousand rooms, the Dalai Lama was bummed out. The stone palace was dark and cold—like a dungeon—and his family didn't live there. Worst of all, there were no other kids. His playmates were old monks, and he made pets out of the mice that lived in his room!

The Dalai Lama lived this lonely life until he was fifteen. That's when his country was invaded by China, and he had to grow up fast. For hundreds of years, Tibet and China had argued about whether Tibet was its own country or just part of China. In 1950, China settled the debate by invading Tibet. The teenage Dalai Lama, who was still training to lead the country, was put in charge two years early to deal with the crisis. He hoped other countries might help, but no one wanted to anger China, a superpower, just to help out tiny Tibet. The Dalai Lama was on his own.

Whenever the Dalai Lama left Potala Palace, he was carried in a small room on poles, called a PALANQUIN, and was followed by a parade of more than one hundred people, the palace horses, and even cages of birds!

━ᘛ━

He struggled to lead his country, but life in Chinese-occupied Tibet got worse and worse for its people.

122

Buddhist temples were destroyed, and hundreds of monks were sent to prison, where many were tortured, starved, and killed. Farmers were sent to work camps, and their lands were given to Chinese immigrants. Although Buddhism forbids violence and Tibet had no army, the people tried to rebel in 1959. They were no match for the huge Chinese army, and their rebellion was crushed.

After the failed rebellion, Tibetans feared that the Chinese would kill their Dalai Lama next, so they surrounded his palace, creating a human shield. It was a weeklong standoff. Even after Chinese soldiers fired shots into the crowd, they still would not leave. The Dalai Lama realized his people would give their lives to protect him. He couldn't just sit by and watch his country fall apart and innocent people die.

> In the years after the Dalai Lama's escape, Buddhism and the Tibetan language were outlawed. Punishment for keeping a picture of the Dalai Lama was death! Over a million Tibetans have been killed. When the Dalai Lama left, there were almost 3,000 Buddhist temples in Tibet. Now there are just nine.

He planned a James Bond–style escape. His only hope was to get help from the outside world. But how? The palace was surrounded, Chinese soldiers were everywhere, and he would have to travel for weeks through the frozen Himalayas to get to the nearest country. In the dark of night, disguised as palace guards, he and his advisers sneaked out of the palace and into the crowd. Miraculously, no one recognized their sacred leader without his glasses on!

This was just the beginning of a terrifying two-week horseback journey through enemy territory. The hard travel, lack of sleep, and bad food soon took its toll: most of the party got very sick, including the Dalai Lama. He was so ill that he couldn't walk, and he had to be strapped onto the back of a yak to finish the trip.

When they finally crossed the border into India, the Dalai Lama knew his adventure was over and the real work was just beginning. He founded a Tibetan community in the town of Dharamsala, high

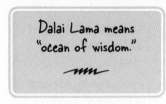

Dalai Lama means "ocean of wisdom."

in the Indian Himalayas, a place where he and his people could practice their religion freely for the first time in ten years. In 1963 he also created a new and improved Tibetan government and their first democratic constitution.

More than fifty years have passed since the Dalai Lama's escape, and Tibet is still not free. Chinese immigrants now outnumber Tibetans, and the country's ancient religion and traditions are practiced only by the escaped Tibetans now living in Dharamsala. The Dalai Lama has spent the past five decades traveling the world to protest this injustice. In 1989 the world heard his message: he was awarded the Nobel Peace Prize. Overall, the Dalai Lama has been presented with more than 125 awards and honors for his peace work. Because of his example, world leaders, Hollywood celebrities, and the media regularly speak out for Tibet and put pressure on China to change their policies.

In 1996, a Seattle, Washington, boy was discovered to be the reincarnation of a Tibetan lama. At age two, the boy was taken to a Buddhist monastery in Nepal to begin his studies.

While he has not achieved all of his goals, the Dalai Lama *has* saved the soul of his people. His Tibetan community in India is thriving, and in spite of China's power, the world knows about Tibet's struggle. In a world that often seems to be filled with war and hatred, the Dalai Lama reminds us that we *can* resolve our conflicts peacefully, if we choose to. The boy who grew up trapped inside a palace has spent the rest of his life traveling the world and spreading his message of peace. One of his teachings says:

The problems we face today—violent conflicts, destruction of nature, poverty, hunger, and so on—are mainly problems created by humans. They can be resolved—but only through human effort, understanding, and the development of a sense of brotherhood and sisterhood.[9]

HOW WILL YOU ROCK THE WORLD?

On every walk I take through a city, I turn a corner and see a homeless person sleeping, doing drugs, or begging. Some people see druggies, beggars, and pests. I see people who have been given up on and have nothing to live for. When I see homeless people, I wish they had a place to live and that they could feel wanted and loved. This is what has made me want to make a home for the homeless.

SAM BUGAS ☼ AGE 13

Elvis Presley

1935–1977 ✧ KING OF ROCK 'N' ROLL ✧ UNITED STATES

Before Elvis there was nothing.

—JOHN LENNON

The young singer gripped his guitar, but his hands still shook. Man, was he nervous! He looked around at the acoustic tiles on the ceiling, the tiles on the walls, the big microphone in front of him. He couldn't get over it. . . . He was finally in the famous Sun Recording Studio. Sure, he had paid the studio four dollars to make a record for his mom's birthday. Sure, they didn't know who he was. But this was *Sun Records*, where the most famous country and blues stars recorded. Anyone could be listening. Maybe this would be his big break.

"Who do you sound like?" asked the woman in the recording booth. "I don't sound like nobody," he answered with a grin. She chuckled at the sweaty teen with his weird long hair and sideburns, but as he belted out the songs, his gravelly voice grew on her. On a piece of scratch paper she scrawled: *Good ballad singer. Hold.*

After he left, a woman in the waiting room asked her, "Who was that singing?"

"I don't know," she answered, "Just some kid."

"Well, whoever he is, he gives me goose bumps!"

She wouldn't be the last woman to get goose bumps from listening to Elvis Presley. Soon he would become the most famous singer the world had ever heard. Women would scream and tear their hair out whenever he opened his mouth. This nervous, greasy-haired kid would become the King of Rock 'n' Roll.

The King grew up dirt poor. The Presleys lived in a two-room "shotgun shack" (named because you could open the front and back door and shoot straight through the house) in Tupelo, Mississippi. His mother, Gladys, worked picking cotton, and his father, Vernon, did odd jobs whenever

> In high school, Elvis joined the football team. He was six feet tall and fast, and he tackled hard, but he hated how the helmet messed up his cool hairdo, so he quit.

he could find the work. One January night in 1935, Gladys went into labor as sleet rained down. She was too poor to afford good medical care, and her baby, Jesse Garon, died in the early morning hours. As the doctor was getting ready to leave, he was shocked to discover a second baby on the way. Just as Elvis was born, the black clouds over Tupelo parted and the morning sun shined through. The Presleys were sure it was a sign: God must have a plan for their son.

Even as a toddler, Elvis loved music. He lived in a mostly black community and grew up listening to his neighbors' music. Gladys also took her son church hopping on Sundays to hear the beautiful gospel music of the South. "Some of those spirituals had big, heavy rhythm beats like a rock-and-roll song," Elvis said later, describing how church music influenced him.

Tragedy hit the Presleys when Elvis was still a young boy. The family was so poor that Vernon resorted to forging checks to pay the bills. He got caught and went to prison. "He only did it because we were hungry," Gladys cried when the police took him away. Elvis and his mother moved in with relatives, and money was tighter than ever. Music became Elvis's escape. He sneaked into honky-tonk bars to listen to black musicians play the blues. Back home, he sang and banged on a cardboard guitar he made himself. "Oh, honey, it could set your teeth to hurtin'!" is how an uncle described Elvis's first singing attempts.

For his eleventh birthday, Elvis begged his parents for a bike. They couldn't afford it, so they bought him a $7.95 guitar instead. With the new guitar, there was no stopping Elvis: he played for whoever would listen. In grade school, he sang in talent contests and wowed an audience of two hundred at the state fair. He even sat outside a local radio station, singing along with the records, until the DJ invited him in. He was so impressed by Elvis's singing that he let the eleven-year-old perform on his show.

In 1948, the Presleys moved to Memphis, Tennessee, in search of better work. Elvis had no friends, and the kids saw him as a hick from the country who lived on the poor side of town. Throughout high school, he was quiet and kept to himself, rarely speaking in class. No one suspected the country boy had secret dreams of becoming a star.

Even though he was a loner, Elvis stood out from the crowd. While the style for guys then was a natural-looking crew cut, Elvis had long hair which he dyed jet black and greased back. Popular guys played sports and wore preppy clothes. Not Elvis. In a classroom full of guys wearing jeans, T-Shirts, and penny loafers, Elvis was likely to be spotted spilling out of his chair, dark-haired and dark-eyed, wearing a pink sports coat and pink and black pants, with a look of disdain adorning his face.

When a classmate told him, "You know, those clothes set you apart from everybody," Elvis grinned and said, "That's what I'm after."

After high school graduation, Elvis worked as a truck driver while trying to break into show biz. Less than a

> Elvis loved food. Once he wolfed down eight cheeseburgers, two BLT sandwiches, and three chocolate milkshakes—in one sitting! But his favorite food in the whole world was deep—fried peanut butter and banana sandwiches.
>
> —————

year after making his mother's birthday record, Elvis got his big break. Sun Records had a ballad to record, but no singer. They remembered the kid with the weird sideburns and decided to give him a shot. Nineteen-year-old Elvis couldn't believe it when they called and told him to be there in three hours. Twenty minutes later, the out-of-breath teen was at the studio. He had run all the way.

Elvis panicked when they didn't like his version of the ballad. But he blew them away when he belted out a song called "That's All Right (Mama)." They decided to record it instead. The song's mix of gospel, country, blues, and Elvis's unique voice created a totally new sound. Memphis radio stations ate it up. Phone calls poured in to stations whenever it was played.

> Elvis, who would become one of the most infamous dancers in the world, didn't dance at his own prom. At the end of the night, he confessed to his disappointed date that he didn't know how.

It wasn't long before word of Elvis spread beyond Memphis. As he traveled the South playing radio shows and concerts, he attracted more and more screaming fans. In 1955 RCA Records came calling: they agreed to pay Sun Records $40,000 to get the rising star, with a $5,000 bonus for Elvis. It was the highest amount ever paid for a pop singer, and more money than Elvis had ever seen. But RCA was really taking a gamble.

In 1950s America, adults listened to big band stars like Frank Sinatra and Doris Day. The music was nice, but definitely not radical. There was a new kind of music out there—*rock 'n' roll*—but it was performed mostly by black artists like Chuck Berry, Little Richard, and Fats Domino. Most white Americans didn't know about rock 'n' roll because white radio stations refused to play black musicians. Teenagers were hungry for something new ... something more dangerous. Elvis hit the scene at the perfect time. *Everything* about him was different and rebellious—his clothes, his hair, his music, and even his dancing. Musician Bob Dylan said, "Hearing him for the first time was like busting out of jail." Elvis was as controversial back then as Lady Gaga is now, and parents hated him just as much.

Just after turning twenty-one, Elvis recorded his first single with RCA, "Heartbreak Hotel." Although most of the RCA executives hated the song and called it a sure "bomb," they released it anyway—and their gamble paid off. "Heartbreak Hotel" hit number one on the charts and sold over a million copies. Elvis was flooded with invitations to all the top television shows. But it was America's number-one program, *The Ed Sullivan Show*, that made him a star.

With fifty-four million people watching, the almost-famous singer strummed his guitar and growled, "I'm ready to rock and roll." The teenage studio audience went wild—guys stomped and howled while girls screamed and pulled their hair! But when the parents watching the show saw Elvis, with his long hair and bad-boy attitude, they really lost it. His dancing was so outrageous that the cameras would only show him from the waist up. It looked as if uncontrollable spasms were running up and down both his legs. This caused the midsection of his body to jolt and shake as if he were being electrocuted.

He was ridiculed as "Elvis the Pelvis" and "unspeakably vulgar."

Yet by the end of the show, host Ed Sullivan was won over by Elvis's polite Southern charm and told his millions of viewers, "This is a real decent, fine boy." Elvis was paid a record $50,000 for three appearances, but more important, Sullivan's comments helped calm parents and critics.

> Once in the middle of the night, Elvis flew a group of friends to Colorado in his private jet just so they could try his favorite Fool's Gold Sandwich: a full loaf of bread stuffed with peanut butter, grape jelly, and fried bacon! One sandwich, by itself, had 42,000 calories.

Just as his singing dreams were coming true, Elvis's other dream—to be a movie star—was also taking off. In 1956 he filmed his first movie, *Love Me Tender*. The movie and title song were hits, and Elvis was in heaven. Over the next ten years, Elvis starred in dozens of movies—including *King Creole*, *G.I. Blues*, *Blue Hawaii*, and *Viva Las Vegas*—and while most of them were silly musicals, they were popular and made piles of money.

After years of struggling in poverty, Elvis was a millionaire. And man, did he enjoy spending his money! He bought closets full of clothes and dozens of cars. But buying his Memphis mansion, Graceland, made him the happiest. His mother, father, and grandmother moved in and filled the yard with eight ducks, two peacocks, one turkey, two pigs, and four donkeys!

In 1958, at the height of his stardom, Elvis got drafted into the army. Most people expected him to get special treatment, like an easy job entertaining the troops, but Elvis wanted to be treated like everybody else. After years of being the outsider, he just wanted to be one of the guys. He even cut his famous hair into a crew cut. On the base in Germany, Elvis worked hard to earn the other soldiers' respect. His superior said, "I had ninety-six guys under my supervision, and none better than Presley."

While Elvis was in the army, in 1961, his mom died. Elvis, who was extremely close to his mother, was overcome with grief and guilt for being so far away during her last days. But it was during this time of grief that Elvis met his future wife: Priscilla Beaulieu, who was then the fourteen-year-old daughter of an army captain stationed in Germany. Elvis finished his army duty, and in 1967, just after Priscilla turned twenty, they married. Their daughter, Lisa Marie, was born a year later.

Everyone wanted to be like Elvis. After he joined the army, enlistment went up by 25 percent!

By the 1970s, Elvis's show biz life began to take its toll. Always on the road, always performing, his marriage fell apart. His high-fat diet led to a severe weight problem—he ballooned from a slim 160 pounds to over 300! And due to his nonstop touring and physically demanding shows, Elvis experienced chronic back pain and problems falling asleep. Doctors prescribed powerful sleeping pills and pain medication to keep him going. Soon Elvis was addicted. Although his friends and family worried about him, he refused to stop working. Elvis loved to perform and told them, "I hope I die on the stage."

On August 16, 1977, at age forty-two, his body gave out, not on stage, but at home. He died and was buried at the Forest Hills

Cemetery in Memphis, next to his grandmother and father. Tens of thousands of fans lined up for hours to pass by his grave and say good-bye. After grave robbers tried to steal Elvis's body, his grave was moved to Graceland. His final resting place is in the meditation garden there.

The outsider from Tupelo lived his life to the fullest and got everything he ever dreamed of: fame, riches, and respect. The shotgun shack where he was born is now a historic monument. Graceland sees six hundred thousand visitors per year and is one of the five most popular house tours in America. The road that passes in front of it is now called Elvis Presley Boulevard.

Elvis poured his heart and soul into his songs, which are some of the most famous ever written—"Don't Be Cruel," "Hound Dog," "Blue Suede Shoes," "All Shook Up," "Jailhouse Rock," "Are You Lonesome Tonight?" He was the first to break down the barriers between black and white music, and he changed the music world forever. Without Elvis, who knows, you might still be listening to bebop instead of hip-hop. He was truly the King of Rock 'n' Roll.

> Elvis decorated Graceland's 18 rooms just how he wanted. His Jungle Room had green carpet on the floor, walls, and even the ceiling; there was also an indoor waterfall and furniture made out of animal horns.

ROCK ON!

JUSTIN BIEBER

When twelve-year-old Justin Bieber won second place in Stratford Idol, a local talent show in Canada, he decided to post some videos of himself singing on YouTube so he could share with his family and friends. He recorded remakes of songs by music icons like Usher and Stevie Wonder, but he added his own spin. It didn't take long before millions of other people were watching his videos too. When his manager saw one of the videos, he signed him almost immediately. Now, Justin Bieber is a household name, and he's still got a lot of time to keep rocking the music world.

Bruce Lee

1940–1973 ◎ MARTIAL ARTIST AND ACTOR
CHINA AND UNITED STATES

When I look around I always learn something, and that is to always be yourself . . . express yourself, and have faith in yourself.

—BRUCE LEE

The nighttime rain plastered Bruce Lee's hair to his head. He stood glaring at another twelve-year-old boy on the dark rooftop of his school. His fists were clenched tight as the other boy laughed and taunted him. A crowd began to gather, and a few boys scrambled up the side of the building to catch a glimpse of the standoff. The Chinese boys gathered behind Bruce and faced a growing gang of angry British boys.

"Hong Kong isn't yours," shouted one of the Chinese, and the two sides broke loose. Bruce dodged and ducked. He could see his friends fighting all around him—fists and feet were flying. He managed to land just one good punch before he got hit himself. As he blacked out, Bruce's last thought was, "I better learn how to defend myself."

This wasn't a scene from a famous kung fu movie. No, this was one of Bruce Lee's first real-life experiences with martial arts.

In 1940, in San Francisco's Chinatown, a baby was born in the year of the dragon and the hour of the dragon—a double symbol of amazing luck and power to the Chinese. He was called Bruce Lee in English, but his Chinese name, Jun Fan, hinted at his future. It meant "to shake foreign countries."

Bruce and his parents moved to Hong Kong, where his parents were from, when he was a baby, and soon their apartment was crowded with four more children. It became even more crowded when an aunt moved in with her five children, a maid, and assorted fish, cats, and dogs! Bruce bounced from crowded room to crowded room with such energy that his family nicknamed him Mo Si Ting, or "never sits still." The only thing that could keep the wild boy in one place was a good book, which he devoured in spite of his thick glasses.

Bruce's father was a performer in the famous Cantonese Opera, so Bruce grew up around actors. He was just three months old when he first appeared in a film! By age eighteen, Bruce had appeared in over twenty Chinese movies. Audiences called him Little Dragon Lee and loved him for his vivid expressions and intense emotion. But the attention for these small roles was nothing compared to the fame that would come later.

> Bruce had so much energy, he couldn't keep still even while he was asleep. He often climbed down from his bunk bed and strolled around the apartment... sleepwalking!

During Bruce's teen years, tensions were high in Hong Kong. The British had colonized the island, and many Chinese people were angry. They experienced plenty of racism from the colonizers, and fights between British and Chinese boys were common. After twelve-year-old Bruce took a beating in a brawl, he decided to learn martial arts.

In Hong Kong it was as common for boys to learn kung fu as it was for American boys to learn baseball. For five years, Bruce studied kung fu six hours a day, seven days a week. When he turned seventeen, he landed his first major role in *Ren hai gu hong* (*The Orphan*), a Chinese movie about a troubled kid. In the movie Bruce got to show off his fighting skills. It was a success, and soon he was offered more action roles. His mother, however, was against her son working in action-packed movies. Bruce had been in trouble at school for bad behavior, and she was anxious about his fighting. After a lot of worrying, she sent him to the United States to live with friends. When Bruce took off for America, he was eighteen years old and had nothing but $100 in his pocket and butterflies in his stomach.

> Bruce was lightning fast. He once put a dime in a reporter's hand and told him to close his fist before he could grab the dime. The reporter closed his hand fast, but when he opened his fist again, the dime was gone. He had a penny instead! Bruce moved so fast, the reporter didn't even see him.

He moved in with his parents' friends in Seattle, Washington, and worked at their restaurant as a busboy. Between work, kung fu practice, and high school, Bruce taught martial arts to his friends. When he started college at the University of Washington, he had so many students that he launched his own martial arts school.

Bruce had a different kind of fight on his hands when he fell in love. Linda Emery was white, and in the 1960s, mixed-race relationships were not accepted. But Bruce and Linda were in love, and they got married anyway. Soon they had a baby boy named Brandon and moved to San Francisco, where Bruce opened another martial arts school.

Bruce's kung fu reputation grew, and it wasn't long before Hollywood discovered him. While he won some roles, including the role of Kato, the kung fu–fighting chauffeur on the television series *The Green Hornet*, Bruce was frustrated with the racism he found in the show-biz industry. There were very few roles for Asian actors, and even roles that were written for Asians were often given to white actors instead.

His acting career stalled when he injured his back in 1970. Doctors told him he would never be able to do martial arts again, but Bruce ignored them and pushed himself to recover. While he was stuck in bed, he wrote his philosophy of fighting, which he called *Jeet Kune Do*.

The philosophy covers both the physical techniques to Bruce's brand of kung fu and how to find inner harmony through the martial arts. It is now a bestselling book called *Tao of Jeet Kune Do*.

Discouraged by Hollywood's prejudice against Asians, Bruce returned to Hong Kong to make films. He was surprised to discover he was already a star there—*The Green Hornet* was a hugely popular television show on the island. Fully recovered from his injury, Bruce made his first hit movie, *The Big Boss*, which became Hong Kong's top-selling movie. Next, he did *The Chinese Connection*, in which he played a martial arts instructor who fights against racist Japanese characters. The success of this movie made Bruce such a star and hero in China that he was able to write, cast, direct, and act in his next movie, *The Way of the Dragon*.

Now it was Hollywood's turn to come crawling back. American producers who had told Bruce he was "too Asian" before were now begging him to star in their movies. He filmed just one American film, *Enter the Dragon*, but sadly never got to see it on the big screen. Just after filming, Bruce collapsed from a severe headache. Doctors told him it was caused by a mysterious swelling of his brain. He later took a pill to fix the headache and went to sleep. He never woke up. Bruce had no idea that he was allergic to the pill. It caused his brain to swell again and killed him. He died at age thirty-three, right at the peak of his career.

Some fans call *Enter the Dragon* the most famous kung fu movie ever made. With his courage and talent, Bruce practically invented the kung fu movie, paved the way for minority actors in Hollywood, and opened doors for current action stars like Jackie Chan and Jason Statham. With his creation of a new kung fu philosophy, Jeet Kune Do, Bruce also revolutionized how people think about the martial arts. Bruce never let other people's prejudices stand in the way of his dreams. He opened the minds of audiences around the world and truly lived up to his name "to shake foreign countries."

In *Enter the Dragon*, Bruce never actually hit his opponents. He missed them by centimeters. In recording sound for the movie, they snapped chicken bones to sound like a punch or kick.

HOW WILL YOU ROCK THE WORLD?

I am going to rock the world by becoming an actor. I think I am really good at acting and that it will be a good career. My hero is Jackie Chan because he is so cool and funny. I want to become an actor because I grew up on movies.

MICHAEL MCGONEGAL AGE 12

Pelé

1940– ◦ ATHLETE ◦ BRAZIL

If Pelé had not been born a man, he would have been a ball.

—BRAZILIAN JOURNALIST

Dust was flying at the construction site, but it wasn't from the jackhammers—a fierce soccer game was going on. Four grown men were huffing and puffing, sweat pouring down their faces as they tried to catch the small barefoot boy with the ball who was heading for their goal.

From the sidelines, a well-dressed man watched. One defender lunged toward the ball, but the boy flicked it over his foot and easily continued toward the goal. As he outran the other men, one tried an illegal slide tackle from behind. But it was as if the boy had eyes in the back of his head—just before the man slid into his heel, the boy dodged right and slammed the ball with his left foot into the space between two barrels. Goal! The observer, who was actually a scout for professional soccer teams, shook his head in amazement.

"Who's the kid?" he asked a worker.

"They call him Pelé."

That eleven-year-old boy would one day become the most famous, highest-paid athlete in the world. He was so beloved that fans would bow down before him, shouting *"El Rey! El Rey!"* (the King) when he entered the stadium.

Pelé was born in 1940 in a small Brazilian town, the son of a former soccer player. His full name was Edson Arantes do Nascimento. Because soccer is Brazil's national sport, most Brazilian boys dream of becoming soccer players. Pelé was no exception. But his family couldn't afford to buy him a ball, so his father stuffed an old sock full of rags and began teaching his son to play. By age five, Pelé was running wild in the streets, kicking his sock into makeshift goals.

> While in school, Pelé earned extra money shining shoes and selling peanuts outside movie theaters.

School bored Pelé. He often played hooky and practiced soccer instead. By the fourth grade, Pelé had missed so much school that he got kicked out. Fine with him ... more time for soccer. He got a job as a cobbler (someone who fixes shoes), earning two dollars a month. But more important, he was able to play soccer on his lunch break and after work with other workers in the neighborhood. The games were rough—no one called fouls, and everyone played barefoot. Pelé loved it. He would return home from a day of working and playing soccer and be too tired to eat dinner.

Although Pelé was the youngest player, he was far better than the older guys. Gossip about the talented kid attracted Waldemar de Brito, one of Brazil's soccer stars and a recruiter for several teams. He watched Pelé play one day at a construction site and was blown away: "I couldn't believe that such a young boy was able to perform some of the moves and tricks with the ball that Pelé was doing."

De Brito coached the boy for several years, and when Pelé turned sixteen, de Brito decided he was ready for the big time: a tryout for a professional team. As Pelé auditioned for the Santos soccer team, de Brito bragged to the coaches, "This boy will be the greatest soccer player in the world." Pelé didn't let him down. While Pelé showed off his moves, the other players stopped practicing and stared in amazement.

Santos signed him up that very day, and in his first season, sixteen-year-old Pelé became the top scorer in the league—a title he held for years.

Though still young and inexperienced, Pelé's greatest wish was to represent his country in the 1958 World Cup. Few people thought he had a chance of making the national team since Brazil was a long shot to win and couldn't afford to take any chances. To everyone's surprise, Brazil took a chance. "I cried with joy when I got the news," Pelé said.

Against the odds, Brazil fought its way into the finals, thanks to Pelé's constant scoring. In Brazil's final game against Sweden, Pelé had his back to Sweden's goal when he chest-trapped a pass. In an amazing gymnastic move, Pelé let the ball drop to his foot, chipped it over his shoulder, then flipped his body around and kicked the ball hard into the net before it could ever touch the ground! The Swedish goalie was so stunned, all he could do was cheer along with the thousands of ecstatic fans. "I've never seen anything like that before and I doubt if I ever will . . . again," the goalie said afterward. "It was unbelievable." Many people still claim Pelé's goal against Sweden is one of the most spectacular goals ever scored in the history of the World Cup. After the game, he was voted the top player in Brazil. At seventeen, Pelé was a soccer legend.

He led his team to victory in two more World Cups (1962 and 1970), making Pelé the only person ever

> When rumors started that the Santos team was being offered a fortune to trade Pelé to another country's team, the Brazilian government actually declared Pelé a national treasure, and therefore non-exportable to a foreign team.

> Pelé, which has no meaning in the Brazilian culture, is a nickname his soccer buddies called him. He always hated it and preferred to be called Edson.

to win three World Cups. He also helped Santos win nine out of the next eleven national championships in Brazil. Before Pelé, people thought it was impossible for anyone to score a thousand goals. But during his twenty-two-year career, Pelé did the impossible, scoring 1,281 goals! That's like a baseball player hitting sixty home runs every year for twenty-two years.

Why, you might be wondering, was Pelé so incredible? Hard work was a big part of it. If Pelé felt he hadn't played his best, he would stay after a game and practice alone for hours. These thousands of hours of solitary practice helped him perfect his deadly accurate kicks, increase his speed, and master his countless tricks.

> Brazilians take soccer very seriously. When they lost the 1966 World Cup, the country went into mourning: black flags hung from every window, and many bridges were closed to prevent suicide attempts.
>
> —m—

Pelé did have a few secret weapons. It seemed to his fans that he must have ESP; he always seemed able to predict just what the other player was about to do. Pelé's ability was so unusual, Brazilian scientists actually studied him and found that his reaction time was a half second faster than a normal human's, and his peripheral vision (the ability to see next to and behind you, while looking forward) was 25 percent stronger than the average Joe's. This superhuman vision let Pelé pass to a teammate on the side while looking straight ahead, fooling his opponents.

> Pelé's experience as a cobbler came in handy for soccer. He often repaired his own soccer shoes, as well as those of his teammates.
>
> —m—

Few soccer players, if any, are able to stay at the top of their game for more than five years, but Pelé played the world's best soccer for an incredible twenty-two years! Today's soccer stars don't even dream of scoring fifty goals in a season. However, in 1974, he scored fifty-two goals. Since he had already scored over a hundred goals in three different seasons, this

142

measly fifty-two goals told him it was time to retire. He was already a multimillionaire and had achieved his wildest boyhood dreams. He played again briefly from 1975 to 1977, when the New York Cosmos offered him $2.8 million per year to join their team for a three-year contract and promote soccer in the United States. He led the team to the US Championship, and then retired at thirty-eight, for good.

Pelé was the greatest soccer player the world has ever known, and some fans would argue he was the greatest athlete in history. His incredible talents brought soccer into the spotlight and introduced the world's most popular sport to the United States, where it thrives today. In 1980, international journalists named him Sportsman of the Century, and in 1994 Brazil appointed him its Minister of Sports. In 1998 he was inducted into the World Sports Humanitarian Hall of Fame, and his footprints are immortalized at the Maracana Stadium in Rio de Janeiro, Brazil. Although no longer playing soccer, Pelé stays active writing books, acting, composing music, and managing his own international business empire.

> Pelé announced his retirement by picking up the ball in the middle of a game and kneeling in the midfield, as if in prayer.

HOW WILL YOU ROCK THE WORLD?

I will make new scientific discoveries that will change the world for the better. I will also play soccer for peace and make movies that will impact people's thoughts. I will write novels that will change the way people see things. This is how I will rock the world.

BRENDAN WATHEN · AGE 13

Bob Dylan

1941– ◦ SINGER ◦ UNITED STATES

*"Master poet, caustic social critic, and intrepid,
guiding spirit of the counterculture generation . . .
Bob Dylan couldn't wait for the music to change.
He couldn't be only part of the change.
He was the change itself."*

—*TIME* MAGAZINE

The Golden Chords took their place backstage with the other talent-show hopefuls. The tap dancers, acrobats, and the girl with her accordion all looked the three young boys up and down with doubt. What were these scrawny thirteen-year-olds up to in their flashy gold jackets? Walking out onstage, the guys in the Golden Chords were nervous, but none more than Bob Zimmerman. He had recently developed a tic in his leg that acted up under stress. As the small audience clapped politely, Bob's leg began to thump the ground wildly. *Oh no*, he thought. But as they launched into their version of the Little

Richard song "Jenny, Jenny," the music possessed him. Bob cut loose, screaming and banging on the piano keys.

The band totally lost themselves in their song—their anxiety, and even the crowd, faded away. When they finished and snapped out of the zone, they fully expected screaming fans and a standing ovation. Instead, the crowd clapped politely again, smirks on their faces. Apparently Hibbing, Minnesota, in 1957 was just not ready for Bob Zimmerman (later known as Bob Dylan) and his revolutionary rock and roll.

At Hibbing Junior High, everyone who was anyone played in the school band. Twelve-year-old Bob went out and bought himself a trumpet. He played and played for days, but he couldn't make anything close to a pleasant noise come from the horn. So he traded the trumpet in for a saxophone. It was even worse. Bob returned that too. After trying two more failed instruments, Bob rented a cheap guitar. It changed his world. He experimented with the six strings for hours, until his fingers were raw. Eventually, the guitar became Bob's sidekick and confidante. He was rarely seen without it hanging across his shoulders.

In the 1950s, Hibbing was a conservative small town. There was only one radio station, and it refused to play music for the youth. Instead, it played what the housewives wanted to hear: polkas and crooners like Frank Sinatra and Bing Crosby. On clear nights, Bob would walk for miles down the Mississippi River carrying his transistor radio just to get reception from the big city rock-and-roll stations.

> Bob's first girlfriend was from the wrong side of the tracks, the adults said, but he didn't care. They loved to dress up—she in leopard-skin tights and red lipstick, and he in a leather hat and popped collar—and walk through downtown Hibbing, causing a stir.

But the times, they were a-changin'. When Bob was sixteen, a new radio station popped up in Hibbing, and once a week it broadcast a DJ named Jim Dandy, whose show was wired in from Virginia. He played blues greats like Howlin' Wolf and Lightnin' Hopkins, two black

145

performers whose music had never rocked the Hibbing airwaves before. Bob was such a fan of the show that he borrowed his father's car to make a pilgrimage to meet Jim Dandy.

When they finally met, Bob was amazed to find out that Jim "Dandy" Reese was a black man! Reese had slipped through the color lines of 1950s radio. He was an inspiration to Bob, who had been punished by his father for "singing black." For the next year, Bob went on several road trips to see his new friend. Reese introduced Bob to a whole new world of music. This was the world that would later inspire him to redefine the roots of folk music. As an adult, Bob would often sing of the injustices done to blacks and other oppressed minorities in 1960s America.

After graduating from high school, Bob left Hibbing as fast as he could to go to college in Minneapolis. There he found kindred spirits. He hooked up with a growing group of political activists who hung out sipping coffee and playing folk music in a hip area called Dinkytown.

One of Bob's songs, "Hurricane," told the story of Rubin "Hurricane" Carter, a black man wrongfully accused and jailed for murder. Rubin's story was made into a movie called THE HURRICANE, starring Denzel Washington.

In the late 1950s and early '60s, folk music was the voice of protest. The songs expressed young people's frustrations with injustice and with the government, which they saw as old, corrupt, and useless. In Dinkytown Bob got his first taste of this powerful music and launched his new life as a folk singer by changing his name to Bob Dylan.

But Bob was too big, even for Dinkytown. He soon hit the road and found himself in New York City. In 1960, New York's Greenwich Village folk music scene was going crazy. Eighteen-year-old Bob was determined to become the greatest folk singer of all time and had his eye on the prize: a record deal with one of the big labels. He played gigs at tiny coffeehouses for $15 a day, sometimes playing until four in the morning.

It wasn't until Bob began writing his own songs that he finally hit the big time. Up to that time, no one in folk music wrote original songs.

It was sacrilege—like writing a new national anthem! But Bob had serious nerve. At his first big gig, opening for blues giant John Lee Hooker, Bob started out by singing two Woody Guthrie songs, and then he launched into his own (gasp!) original tune called "Song for Woody." Some people were impressed, but many were horrified. When a glowing review came out in the *New York Times*, praising Bob's "genius," there was a big buzz on the street. Good or bad, Bob was changing the face of folk music, and he wasn't even twenty years old! A few months later, Bob's dream came true—he signed a deal with Columbia Records.

His first album, *Bob Dylan*, was unlike anything on the radio at the time. Nowadays, angry protest songs are common. But back in the early '60s, most pop singers sang love songs or light, happy tunes. Not Bob. He wrote songs about the problems he was passionate about: war, racism, and poverty. He wanted to shake people up. He wanted to change the world.

Rumor has it that Bob took his last name from the great twentieth-century poet, Dylan Thomas.

The album flopped, selling just a few hundred copies. Columbia prepared to drop Bob as soon as his contract was up, but his agent at Columbia, John Hammond, flew into a rage, telling the other executives that if they dropped him it would be "over my dead body." Since Hammond actually had a heart condition, Columbia took his threat seriously. They didn't want to lose one of their top executives, so they gave Bob a second chance.

Meanwhile, Bob madly wrote and rewrote. He was determined not to let poor sales get him down. Eventually, he came up with "Blowin' in the Wind," a social commentary that launched him to stardom.

Bob finished the lyrics at a local coffee shop. A friend who was performing there heard Bob tinkering with it during a break and grabbed the lyrics from him. "Ladies and gentlemen," he said from stage, "I'd like to sing a new song by one of our great songwriters. It's hot off the pencil, so here it goes." When he finished "Blowin' in the Wind," the entire crowd jumped to their feet and cheered. When the song was released on a later album, it became the first of many Bob Dylan hits.

Soon Bob was famous, and his songs were being sung all across America and even around the world. But by age twenty-five, he was burned out; the pressures of stardom were too much for him. He disappeared from the music scene for four years! The official story was that Bob had a motorcycle accident and was recovering. No one really knows if the story was true or an excuse to escape his crazy rock-star life.

True or not, the time out of the spotlight was good for Bob. He and his wife had two kids, and fatherhood rejuvenated him, giving him a new sense of joy. Bob's disappearance didn't hurt his fame, either. In fact, he just got more popular! After all, he wasn't just a famous singer/songwriter, he was also *mysterious*. Bob made a triumphant return to the spotlight in 1968 to honor his idol Woody Guthrie at a memorial concert. After that, he played all kinds of different music, branching into electric guitar rock and roll and then returning to one of his first loves, the blues.

Bob's son, Jakob Dylan, is the lead singer of The Wallflowers (named for a tune Bob wrote in 1971). Jakob's popular song "Hand Me Down" is about growing up in the shadow of his famous father.

Bob Dylan's music is still played around the world, and he continues to record and perform today. As a boy he dreamed of making a difference through his music. His songs of protest have made such a difference that Bob has been nominated for the Nobel Prize in Literature repeatedly since 1996. The Nobel committee praised him:

His blend of poetry and social consciousness with music is entirely appropriate for Nobel recognition. His songs . . . have been passionately concerned with civil rights, world peace, the preservation of the environment, and other crucial global causes.

Bob Dylan's music still inspires passion, frustration, beauty, and change in listeners, reminding us all to make our own difference in the world.

ROCK ON!

YUTO MIYAZAWA

When he was three years old, Yuto Miyazawa saw his father playing guitar and decided he wanted to learn too. In fact, all he wanted to do was play guitar. Before long, he had completely surpassed his father's ability and was playing advanced-level metal songs. When he was nine, he was featured playing Ozzy Osbourne's "Crazy Train" on *The Ellen Degeneres Show*. After the crowd settled down following the amazing performance, Ellen had a surprise for him: Ozzy was there to meet him! At this rate, he'll be revolutionizing music just like Ozzy and Bob Dylan did.

Chico Mendes

1944–1988 ◈ ACTIVIST ◈ BRAZIL

Chico Mendes was a butterfly flapping his wings over the forest. He started a storm that is still rising above the Amazon, a storm that may yet break across the world.

—DR. STEPHAN SCHWARTZMAN, ANTHROPOLOGIST WITH ENVIRONMENTAL DEFENSE

The enormous crash of a falling tree shook the ground as they walked. Chico yelled to the group of fifty following him, "Don't worry, friends, we'll be OK. But please watch out for falling branches." The buzzing of chainsaws grew louder as they made their way through the thick rainforest. The people following Chico were mostly rubber tappers who lived and depended on this land that had been taken from them and was now being destroyed.

As they approached the clear-cut site, the sound of chainsaws was deafening. They could see what looked like a cemetery, the charred, blackened tree stumps jutting out from the barren earth. They could also see a man with a gun guarding the area. His orders were to shoot anyone who tried to stop the cutting. Chico's unarmed group kept walking toward the destruction, hoping they looked braver than they felt. They stuck close together, the women squeezing their children's hands to give them courage.

"Please stop!" a marcher yelled over the noise. The guard and the loggers turned and stared in amazement. *What were women and children doing here?* Pointing his gun at the group, the guard ordered them to leave. They didn't move. Tension hung in the air as the minutes ticked by and everyone waited to see what would happen. Finally, the guard dropped his gun. He didn't care if his boss fired him; he couldn't shoot women and children.

> Twenty-five percent of the drugs we use in the Western world contain rainforest products, yet only 1 percent of rainforest plants have been studied for their medical uses.

The loggers shut off their giant saws and walked out into the jungle. The cutting was over.

Chico Mendes led many of these peaceful protests, called *empates*. He inspired the people who lived and worked in the jungles of Brazil to rise up and fight for their land and their way of life, and his courage led the way for the environmentalists who followed in his footsteps.

The Brazilian rainforest, where Chico grew up, is the largest tropical rainforest left on Earth. At 1.2 billion acres, it is equal in size to the ninth largest country in the world. The rainforest gets its name from the abundant rain that falls there. Even in the dry season, rain falls every day. All that rain has helped to create an environment that has more species of plants and animals per square foot than

> One kind of rubber tree has exploding fruit! The fruit flings its seeds more than 50 feet.

anywhere else on Earth. The incredible number of trees in the rainforest breathe in carbon dioxide (a gas pollution that cars and other man-made machines give off) and turn it back into oxygen, which helps keep the Earth's climate healthy.

It is easy to imagine why Chico was so protective of this place. He was born in northwestern Brazil in 1944, and he spent his days playing beneath trees as tall as skyscrapers and chasing butterflies bigger than his head. Chico's parents were rubber tappers, and for them, life in the jungle could be very hard. They got up before sunrise and worked long into the evening.

By age nine, Chico was tapping rubber too. He walked twenty miles a day, tapping between one hundred fifty and two hundred trees. He carefully cut V-shaped lines into each rubber tree's trunk and let the white sap run out into a tin cup he set below (back then, people used this sap to make rubber for tires). During these long walks, Chico grew to appreciate the rainforest and to understand that each part is there for a reason; the animals, the trees, and even the insects play an important role in maintaining the intricate web of life.

> You'd have a hard time breathing without the Amazon rainforest. It is called the "lungs of our planet" because it constantly recycles carbon dioxide (what we breathe out) into oxygen (what we breathe in). It produces more than 20 percent of the world's oxygen!

Wealthy men called rubber barons ran the rubber plantations, but the workers were mostly Amazon Indians and other poor people lured into rubber tapping by the promise of a good life. But the good life never came. The bosses kept workers in debt by paying them next to nothing and overcharging them for food and lodging. For all their long hours, workers usually owed the bosses more money than they earned. They could never get out of debt or save enough to leave, so they became like slaves.

Even if they could leave, most had nowhere else to go. They couldn't read and had no other job skills. The rubber barons didn't want workers learning how to read—if workers were educated, they might figure out how they were being cheated. Chico's father, however, could read a little, and each night, after a long day of work, he taught his son how. When Chico was twelve, a Brazilian journalist named Euclides Tavora visited the Mendes house and was impressed by the boy's reading skills.

He offered to teach Chico, who happily began spending weekends at Tavora's book-filled house.

When Chico was twenty, he started teaching other workers how to read whenever he wasn't tapping rubber trees. He knew the rubber barons were corrupt and that workers had to get educated if they wanted to fight back. Five years later, he quit rubber tapping to teach full-time and also began organizing worker protests.

When a man-made rubber was created in the 1970s, demand for Brazil's natural rubber went down the tubes. The rubber barons had to find another way to make money, so they switched to cattle ranching. They began cutting and burning millions of acres of rainforest to create grazing land for their cows. When a chunk of forest the size of California was burned down, forcing all the people who lived there to leave their homes, Chico knew it was time for drastic action.

He started up the National Council of Rubber Tappers and promoted nonviolent demonstrations. Chico spent years battling the stubborn Brazilian government, trying to get them to protect large portions of the Amazon rainforest where rubber tappers could live. But the ranchers had the government in their pockets. They hardly protected any land at all, and they acted as if Chico and the rubber tappers didn't exist.

In 1987, Chico was invited to the United States by environmentalists concerned about the destruction of the rainforest. He explained how rubber tappers lived without harming the land and asked for help in convincing the Brazilian government to stop further destruction of the land. By then, an area twice the size of California had been destroyed. Burning all that land was causing huge problems. When fires burn, they give off carbon dioxide, a gas that traps heat near the Earth's surface. When too much

> Fifty percent or more of all life forms live in the rainforest!
>
> ᴍᴍ

> The Amazon River flows for thousands of miles through the Brazilian rainforest and holds more types of fish than the entire Atlantic Ocean!
>
> ᴍᴍ

carbon dioxide is released, the planet begins to warm up, causing the ecosystems of plants and animals to suffer. This is called the greenhouse effect.

Chico received two awards for his efforts, one from the United Nations Environmental Program and another from the Better World Society. But when he returned to Brazil after the conferences, the ranchers were extremely angry that Chico had brought world attention to their actions. As the ranchers got angrier, Chico resolved to make more progress. He led more and more *empates* and succeeded in saving more than twenty thousand acres from being burned in 1988 alone.

But just when he was starting to turn things around in Brazil, Chico was shot and killed by a group of ranchers on December 22, 1988. Everyone knew who were responsible for Chico's death, but they were too afraid of them to speak up.

Chico's death made headlines all over the world and brought even more attention to the environmental damage the ranchers were doing to the rainforest. In 1989, several US senators flew to Brazil to talk about environmental programs. Under pressure from the media, the Brazilian government approved a plan to replant 2.5 million acres of deforested land. They also stopped logging in much of the rainforest that Chico had fought for, instead creating nature reserves. They called the first 2.4 million–acre reserve the Chico Mendes Extractive Reserve.

The Amazonian Indian word for rubber tree is caoutchouc, which means "weeping wood."

In 1992, leaders from all over the world met in Brazil for the United Nations Conference on the Environment. Unfortunately, Chico couldn't be there, but all remembered him as the greatest champion and defender of the rain forest. Chico fought his whole life to preserve the land that he loved, and his memory inspires people all over the world to continue in the fight to save the still rapidly disappearing rain forest.

HOW WILL YOU ROCK THE WORLD?

If I could rock the world, I would help build houses in New Orleans or Africa. The reason why I would like to do this is because I'm growing up in two very nice houses. Doing so, this makes me realize how many people aren't as fortunate as me. Another reason I would like to do this is because you need three things in life to survive: water, food, and shelter. If you are missing one of those three things, it can be a very hard lifestyle, and I would like to change that for people.

HENRY MACEACHERN AGE 13

Stephen King

1947– ◦ WRITER ◦ UNITED STATES

King paints a masterful, terrifying picture of every child's (and maybe adult's) worst fear.

—ST. LOUIS POST-DISPATCH

The high school sophomore handed out copies of his latest writing effort, *The Village Vomit*, to classmates and friends. Similar to *MAD Magazine*, Stephen's pseudo-newspaper made fun of everyone at Lisbon Falls High School, from jocks to teachers, cheerleaders to nerds. Stephen thought his stories were hilarious—but would the other kids like it?

He had no need to worry. Filled with fake news items like farting cow contests and faculty characters like Miss Rat Pack and Miss Maggot (real-life teachers Miss RayPach and Miss Margitan)—the *Vomit* was a hit! It wasn't long before everyone in school was reading Stephen's zine and "busting a gut," as he described it. Though most of the teachers could take a joke, "Miss Maggot" was not pleased. Issues of the

Vomit were confiscated and destroyed. Stephen was sent to detention!

Luckily, the principal appreciated Stephen's writing abilities more than his sense of humor. Instead of giving him detention, he arranged for Stephen to write for a real paper, the *Lisbon Enterprise*, covering high school sports. Stephen, who played football, was perfect for the job. He quickly learned the ins and outs of professional writing, and he was happy to earn a penny for each word he wrote. In the future, Stephen King would earn a *lot* more for his writing—in fact, his stories would make him a household name and a millionaire many times over!

> Because Durham was so small, there was no school bus to Lisbon Falls, and Stephen had to ride in a taxi to high school. But it was no ordinary taxi—it was a converted hearse!

Born on September 21, 1947, in the coastal town of Portland, Maine, Stephen King was considered a miracle baby. Doctors told Stephen's mother, Ruth, that she would never be able to give birth, so the baby was an unexpected arrival. When Stephen was two, his father left, and it was up to his mother to support the family single-handedly. Over the next ten years, they moved a lot—Indiana, Connecticut, Wisconsin . . . wherever Ruth could find a job. Eventually, they ended up in Durham, Maine, where Ruth cared for Stephen's grandparents. They moved into a two-story farmhouse with no running water. This was the 1950s, but they had to carry all their drinking water in from a well. There wasn't even a bathroom—they had to use an outhouse instead!

> Believe it or not, the King of Horror is terrified of rats, insects, and funerals.

Durham was tiny, with not much going on. Bored and isolated at the farmhouse, Stephen quickly developed a love for comic books. An avid reader herself, Ruth encouraged him to read and write, giving her son a quarter for each story he created. When he was only seven, Stephen wrote his first scary story about a dinosaur taking over a small town. He was particularly drawn to horror comic books, science fiction, and fantasy novels, like *The Lord of the Rings*.

Although he was not the most popular boy, by middle school Stephen was becoming famous for his stories. He wrote one about some students taking over their school and handed out chapters to his classmates as he finished them. They waited on pins and needles, wishing Stephen could write faster. You see, all the characters in the suspenseful story were based on the real kids in his school—and they couldn't wait to find out what they would do next in Stephen's story!

In high school, Stephen was an offensive tackle for the football team and played guitar in a rock band called the MoonSpinners. Though Stephen had other interests in high school, he was still obsessed with writing. He and his best friend, Chris Chelsey, made a book of their horror stories, including doozies by Stephen like "The Cursed Expedition" and "The Thing at the Bottom of the Well." Using a beat-up mimeograph machine, they made copies of their collection, *People, Places, and Things—Volume 1*, to sell. The book's introduction read:

We warn you ... the next time you lie in bed and hear an unreasonable creak or thump, you can try to explain it away ... but try Steve King's and Chris Chelsey's explanation: People, Places, and Things.

Before graduating, Stephen had not only completed his first novel, *The Aftermath*, but had also begun sending his writing to publishers. One of his short stories, "I Was a Teenage Graveyard Robber," got published, and he also won a magazine essay contest.

Stephen then went to the University of Maine, where he was active in student politics and protested the Vietnam War. There he continued writing and even had a weekly column in the college newspaper called "King's Garbage Truck," named for the grab bag of topics he covered. The column gave Stephen a lot of freedom—he wrote about movies, books, politics ... whatever struck his fancy. He also sold another story. *Starling Mystery Stories* paid him thirty-five dollars for "The Glass

Floor." It wasn't much, but Stephen was psyched to be making money from his writing!

But making a *living* as a writer wasn't so easy. After college, Stephen got married and had a daughter, and with a family to support, he took a job at a Laundromat. Fortunately, after a year of washing clothes, Stephen got a job he liked more: teaching high school English. He still found time to write every day, hoping his stories might sell and help pay the bills. He sent his novel *The Running Man* to dozens of publishers, which all rejected it (years later it was made into a movie starring Arnold Schwarzenegger and Sharon Stone). But one editor at Doubleday Publishing thought Stephen had potential and told him to keep sending stories.

Stephen almost didn't. The next book he wrote was *Carrie*, the story of an unpopular girl who uses her telepathic powers to get revenge on teasing classmates. Stephen hated it so much, he threw it in the garbage! Luckily, his wife fished it out and convinced him to send it to Doubleday. They loved it. Stephen almost passed out when he got their telegram: "'Carrie' officially a Doubleday book, $2,500 advance against royalties, congrats, kid—the future lies ahead." The money came just in time—Stephen was broke; he couldn't even afford a phone.

> When Stephen meets with his editors, he likes to do it over hot dogs and peanuts at Yankee Stadium.

He was elated to see his first novel published (and to get a phone!), but $2,500 was still not enough money to quit his day job. Then, in 1973 Doubleday sold the paperback rights for *Carrie* to another company, and Stephen got another surprise. He would get $200,000 for the sale! *Carrie* went on to become one of Stephen's most popular novels, and in 1976, a movie was released, starring Sissy Spacek and John Travolta. According to Stephen, "The movie made the book, and the book made me." Stephen could finally afford to leave his teaching job and write full-time.

Over the next decades, Steven wrote some of the bestselling and scariest stories of all time: *Salem's Lot*, *Cujo*, *IT*, *Pet Sematary*, *The Shining*, and *The Stand*. After the popularity of *Carrie*, each book earned Stephen

> Stephen got the idea for his book PET SEMATARY when his cat Smucky got killed by a car.
>
> ⁓⁓

millions. Instead of the trailer they had once called home, the Kings moved into a 123-year-old mansion, complete with twenty-three rooms and a black iron fence decorated with bats and spider webs. The house is even rumored to be haunted by the ghost of an old army general!

Stephen has written more than eighty books, and many of them are available in more than thirty languages. Many of his stories have been made into movies: *Carrie*, *The Shining*, *Stand by Me*, *The Shawshank Redemption*, and *The Green Mile*, to name a few. Just like his high school classmates, now millions of fans are spellbound by Stephen's tales. But for Stephen King, writing has always been his life's passion, ever since he wrote his first stories for his mom, at a quarter apiece.

ROCK ON!

SAM STERN

Sam Stern started cooking early on when he was helping his mom in the kitchen in England. When he was a teenager, he realized other kids would probably like to cook too, so he wrote a book for them, *Cooking Up a Storm*. "It's full of simple tasty recipes, the sort of things that my mates and I like to eat," Sam said. Since then, he's written four more cookbooks, and he's not even twenty yet! Check them out:

Real Food, Real Fast
Get Cooking
Sam Stern's Student Cookbook
Eat Vegetarian

Stevie WondeR

1950– ◈ SINGER ◈ UNITED STATES

For the audience that has cherished his voice, lyrics, and music for nearly forty years, Stevie Wonder has an ability to see the world like few others of his generation.

—MARK BEYER, BIOGRAPHER

Now clap your hands," Little Stevie Wonder coached the Motortown Revue audience during his live performance of "Fingertips," his first hit song. He bobbed his head with the music as the crowd clapped the beat. "Say 'yeah!'"

"Yeah!" the audience called back, amazed at the musical talent of the "twelve-year-old genius," as the host had dubbed him.

The name Stevie Wonder came from Berry Gordy Jr. at Motown Records, who signed Stevie on and launched his career. There's some debate about Stevie's birth name, though. As the story goes, the hospital records in Saginaw, Michigan, read Steveland Morris, but his father's last name was Judkins and his mother's name was Hardaway, both

> Retrolental fibroplasia, also known as retinopathy of prematurity, affected premature babies from 1941 until 1953, when doctors realized the oxygen was causing it. Now, they have figured out just the right amount of oxygen to give to premature babies so their bodies will develop but their eyes won't be damaged.
>
> ᴍᴍ

last names that Stevie used in years to come. Where the name Morris came from is a mystery, and Stevie has never set the record straight.

While the name is a mystery, some might call Stevie's birth a miracle. His mother had been in constant pain during her pregnancy with him, and when the pangs shot through her entire body, she knew something was terribly wrong. At the hospital, Stevie was born two months premature and only weighed four pounds, about half the weight of a normal newborn baby. The doctors and nurses whisked him away to an incubator, a crib enclosed with plastic to keep out germs and other toxins, until they were sure he was well enough to go home. That incubator saved his life, but it's also what made Stevie Wonder blind.

Doctors didn't know it yet, but the oxygen that they pumped into the incubator to help premature babies finish developing actually damaged the babies' undeveloped eyes. Scar tissue grew in Stevie's eye tissue, and he was forever blinded.

But blindness didn't hold Stevie back. When he was still very young, his family moved from Saginaw, Michigan, to Detroit. Their apartment on the east side was small and lower class, but it was literally musical. Electric-guitar blues music drifted out of the club windows on the street level, and kids on the sidewalks were putting their own spin on it, creating doo-wop. Inside the apartment, Stevie and his two older brothers banged spoons on pots, played harmonica, and sang their own songs. Although Stevie's father was rarely home and almost never showed affection for his family, he bought Stevie a set of bongo drums before he could even walk. Stevie played with them constantly and even slept with them.

Stevie's mom was careful not to hold him back because of his blindness. She believed a boy needed to play outside and with other children to gain confidence and social skills and so other kids wouldn't treat him as though something was wrong with him. Stevie would memorize the number of steps between objects—trees, rocks, the teeter-totter, and the slide—and create a mental map of the places he played. He was just as rambunctious as any boy, and all the other kids wanted to play with him.

When Stevie was nine, he began singing with the church choir, but as much as he liked to sing, he wanted to get his hands on the piano. When he asked the music director if he could play, she happily told him yes, knowing he had a musical gift. Stevie would play the piano for hours between church services, mastering gospel, blues, and whatever other music he felt like playing, and he always drew a crowd. People would sit in the church just to hear Stevie play.

At eleven, Stevie met Ronnie White from The Miracles, who introduced him to Berry Gordy Jr. at Motown Records. In no time, Stevie had two albums, and within two years, the hit song "Fingertips—Pt. 2" could be heard anywhere in the United States.

After a couple years, though, Little Stevie's albums weren't selling very well. The Motown Records executives weren't sure if they should keep Stevie or break their contract with him. When he turned fourteen, they dropped "Little" from his name, and a few years later, Stevie signed a contract to not only perform his own music but also to write songs for other singers. The most famous song he wrote for another artist was "Living for the City" for Ray Charles. Ray was Stevie's role model, so he was honored when Ray sang the song; then he was incredibly proud when Ray's performance of it won a Grammy Award in 1975. Wow!

Also in the seventies, Stevie started his own record label, and he chose to produce songs that were about world concerns—wars, world

> In a lesson to trust her, Stevie's mom once told him not to leave the porch. He was about three years old and didn't think he needed to listen to his mother. He waited until he thought his mom wasn't looking, and he walked off the porch—straight into a pile of dog poo! "I told you," his mom said.

hunger, civil rights, and so on. He won all kinds of Grammys for these songs. He's known for raising money for humanitarian causes like the Paralympics, AIDS treatment, the end of apartheid, and resources for blind children. But in 1972, Stevie was in a terrible car crash, and he was in a coma for four days. When he woke up, he couldn't smell or taste anything, so the only senses he had left were hearing and touch. Fortunately, he got his senses of taste and smell back after a while.

Then in the eighties, Stevie Wonder sold more albums than ever before. *Hotter than July* became a platinum selling album, and then Stevie's version of "Happy Birthday" was used in a tribute to Martin Luther King Jr. Stevie worked together with other artists to create best-selling songs too—"Get It" with Michael Jackson and "Ebony and Ivory" with Paul McCartney were two of the most popular ones. The Rock and Roll Hall of Fame inducted Stevie in 1989, and then in 1996 he won a Lifetime Achievement Award.

> Other famous blind musicians are Ray Charles, Andrea Bocelli, and Jose Feliciano.

Stevie is still a popular recording artist today. He's done duets with some of today's pop stars like Snoop Dogg and Andrea Bocelli. He toured the United States with thirteen concerts in 2007, and in 2008 he played at the Democratic National Convention when Senator Barack Obama accepted the nomination for president.

Stevie Wonder has amazed audiences for more than fifty years. His broad musical style and variety of song topics have earned him numerous awards over the years, but perhaps his most impressive accomplishment is his ability to help people realize that blindness doesn't have to be a disability.

HOW WILL YOU ROCK THE WORLD?

We take walking for granted. Have you ever thought about how it would affect your life if you were paralyzed? I will become a professional basketball player and donate most of the money I own to people who are paralyzed. In my free time I can volunteer to be a visitor, a helper, and a friend. When I retire I will get my masters degree to become a physical therapist. As a physical therapist I plan to help people who are paralyzed.

HUNTER DUPUIS ⚛ AGE 13

Matt Groening

1954– ❈ CARTOONIST ❈ UNITED STATES

Most grown-ups forget what it was like to be a kid.
I vowed I would never forget.

—MATT GROENING

In the back row of the class, Bart Simpson sits hunched over his desk, scribbling a drawing of his dog, Santa's Little Helper, in the margins of his notebook. Mrs. Krabappel walks the aisles menacingly.

"Today, class, I am handing back your multiplication tests. *Most* of you passed. *Some* of you however . . . ," she says, whipping her head around to stare directly at Bart. She is not smiling.

"Bart," she barks, "I don't recall assigning *pet portraits* for last night's homework. Quit it, Michelangelo!"

"Chill out, man," says Bart, continuing his masterpiece. Mrs. Krabappel sighs and sends him to Principal Skinner's office . . . again.

This could be a scene from *The Simpsons*. But it's not. With a few name changes, this was the real-life childhood of Matt Groening (pronounced like "raining"), future creator of that hugely popular animated television show. Sure, he's famous and well-respected now, but back then he was just another kid getting into trouble. A lot.

The Simpsons was inspired by Matt's tortured childhood, which he spent in Portland, Oregon. His dad was a cartoonist and encouraged his son's early doodling habit. Matt doodled his way into high school, drawing cartoons in every class, even PE! He even remembers "injuring himself severely while doodling on the parallel bars." Although Matt's constant cartooning got him into trouble at school, he finally found an outlet for all that energy scribbling around inside him. At fourteen, he started drawing a cartoon strip for his high school newspaper. But just like Bart, Matt's wacky sense of humor got him into trouble, and he eventually got kicked off the newspaper staff. Bet they're sorry now!

After high school, Matt went to Evergreen College in Olympia, Washington. It's hard to say whether he chose the school because of its great art department or because it doesn't give grades. At the time, Matt considered himself more of a writer—he actually thought that he was a lousy cartoonist and that all his friends could draw better than he could. But one friend, fellow cartoonist Lynda Barry (creator of the popular illustrated character Marlys), never let him give up on his art, even when he wanted to quit. Matt kept on doodling, and eventually he got better and better. His simple style is now copied by cartoonists everywhere.

In 1977, after college, Matt packed up and moved to Los Angeles hoping to become a writer. Just as he pulled into town at 2 AM, his car broke down in the fast lane of the

> The streets of Portland, Oregon, scream THE SIMPSONS. There's Flanders Street (Ned Flanders), Lovejoy Street (Reverend Lovejoy), Terwilliger Boulevard (Bob Terwilliger, aka Sideshow Bob), and Quimby Street (Mayor Quimby).

> If you switch the letters around, B-A-R-T actually spells B-R-A-T.

167

Hollywood Freeway. This nightmarish experience inspired another cartoon strip, *Life in Hell*. Instead of sending his friends back in Oregon grouchy letters complaining about Los Angeles, he sent them cartoon strips about how sorry his life was. His main character, Binky, who always moped and complained about how unfair life was, was a rabbit because it was the easiest thing for Matt to draw. When some editors at the newspaper that Matt worked for, the *Los Angeles Reader*, got a look at his strip one day, they thought *Life in Hell* was hilarious. They began running it in the paper, and Matt developed a huge following. Soon you could see *Life in Hell* in 250 newspapers around the world.

In high school, Matt and some buddies formed their own political party called Teens for Decency. They even had a slogan: "If you're against decency, then what are you for?" Matt, who later in life wrote some of the most indecent comedy on television, was actually elected school president on that slogan!

In 1985, a television producer saw *Life in Hell* and asked Matt to draw an animated short for a new comedy show called *The Tracy Ullman Show*. Legend has it that just fifteen minutes before a meeting with the big television executives, Matt was informed that he should show them something new and original. While in the waiting room, he frantically sketched a family of characters, giving them the names of his own family: Homer, Marge, Lisa, Maggie. The only name he changed was his—Matt became Bart. In the meeting, the bigwigs asked what

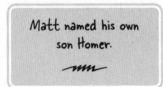

Matt named his own son Homer.

Homer did for a living, and Matt blurted out the first thing that popped into his head: "He works in a nuclear plant." They cracked up, and *The Simpsons* was born.

The original shorts were just two minutes long, and the characters looked quite different from the Simpsons we know today: Bart had lots more spikes on his head, Marge's hair was taller, Lisa just looked silly, and Homer didn't say "D'oh" even once. Audiences weren't crazy about *The Tracy Ullman Show*, but they loved the Simpson family, so Fox gave them their own thirty-minute television show in 1989.

When you take a look at almost any hilarious *Simpsons* script, it's easy to see why Matt considered himself a writer instead of a cartoonist:

From the episode "Bart Gets Famous"
Setting: a factory tour

Bart: Have any of the workers ever had their hands cut off by the machinery?

Guide: No—

Bart: And then the hand started crawling around and tried to strangle everybody?

Guide: No, that has never happened.

Bart: Any popped eyeballs?

Guide: I'm not sure what kind of factory you're thinking of; we just make boxes here.

The Simpsons went down in history as the very first animated show to get a prime-time slot. Fox executives took a chance when they decided to do *The Simpsons* not as an after-school cartoon for kids, but as an evening show for both kids *and* adults. Their gamble paid off. Even though the show has been accused of being obnoxious and offensive, you can bet almost everyone will laugh at Bart's chalkboard messages that start each episode: "I will not trade pants with others," or maybe, "Beans are neither musical nor fruit." Yes, it is rude and crude, but it also makes you laugh until your stomach hurts.

> Bart's voice is done by a girl! Nancy Cartwright has been doing Bart, Nelson, Todd Flanders, and Ralph Wiggum since the show began.

In 1998, another television series Matt Groening had developed was released: FUTURAMA. It's a humorous, science-fiction animated series about life in the year 3000.

—ᴍᴍ—

The Simpsons has won lots of awards, including more than twenty-five Primetime Emmy Awards, almost thirty Annie Awards, and a Peabody Award. As of 2012, the show is still running, and audiences are still laughing. With reruns, it is doubtful the show will ever stop, until *The Simpsons* achieves world domination and Bart becomes ruler of the land. And there will be Matt, wringing his hands and laughing maniacally, just like Mr. Burns.

ROCK ON!

AMAN REHMAN

When he was just three years old, Aman Rehman completed his first computer animation, starring dancing alphabet letters. His father, a poor scooter mechanic, took Aman to Dehra Dun's College of Interactive Arts, where officials laughed at the idea of such a young boy in their classes. When they gave him a chance, though, they were stunned. Within just five months of starting class, he had written his own software program! By the time he was eight, he was teaching adult students at the college how to animate with a computer. He is dedicated and often works on the computer for eight hours a day.

Yo-Yo Ma

1955– ✸ CELLIST ✸ FRANCE AND UNITED STATES

His bow has a voice.

—YO-YO MA'S MOTHER

Concert attendees at the University of Paris held their breath, captivated by the five-year-old music prodigy on the stage. Yo-Yo's fingers danced over the cello strings as he skillfully slid the bow across them with his other hand. He was approaching the end of the first suite of Bach's *Six Suites for Unaccompanied Cello*. He was supposed to stop when he finished the first section, but he found himself picturing the upcoming notes in his head—he'd memorized them the year before. He decided right then to play all six suites, no matter what the concert program said. At the end, the audience was thrilled, and so was Yo-Yo. His first public performance was a good taste for what the rest of his life as a musician would be like.

Yo-Yo Ma's parents were poor musicians. They'd moved to Paris from China to escape the violence of their homeland, but after World

171

War II, it was difficult for anyone to make a living in war-torn France. By the time Yo-Yo was born, his mother was trained in opera, but she wasn't working, and his father had two jobs—teaching music at the University of Paris and giving private music lessons. Yo-Yo, his older sister, and his parents lived in a one-room apartment that didn't even have any heat! But they surrounded themselves with the simple pleasures of classical music, especially Bach and Mozart.

> While many people use the words PITCH and TONE to mean the same thing, they are actually a little different. Pitch is how high or low a sound is. Tone, on the other hand, is the quality of the sound. A musician can be perfectly on pitch, but the tone can still sound bad—raspy, shrill, or piercing.

By the time Yo-Yo could talk, he was making up his own songs—his favorite was about a frog—and he had a keen ear for tone. When he was just three years old, his sister had played in a violin recital, and when she asked Yo-Yo if he'd liked it, he replied, "You played very well. . . . But you were just a little off tone."[9] His parents were amazed— he was right. When they asked him how he knew when the sound was off, he shrugged. He just knew.

But Yo-Yo's parents were nervous about training their son to be a musician. After all, they were both very good musicians and could barely provide food and shelter for their family. Still, they could see Yo-Yo was incredibly talented, and they fretted about stifling his gift. Finally, they decided to teach him music but not to pressure him to do it professionally as he grew older.

As anticipated, Yo-Yo made a very good music student, but he resisted learning the violin, as his father originally proposed. "I don't like the sound violins make," he said. "I want a big instrument."[10] After months of Yo-Yo making this claim, his father brought a small cello to one of their lessons. Yo-Yo was thrilled! From then on, Yo-Yo Ma would be known as a cellist.

When Yo-Yo was seven, his father spent all his savings to fly his family to the United States to visit his brother. Although they were in New York to take care of family business, Yo-Yo's father took the opportunity to set up three concerts for his children. Just like at the University of Paris concert, everybody loved Yo-Yo. After the second concert, Yo-Yo's father was reveling in the success of his children's performance when a representative from the Trent School in New York City approached him and offered him a job teaching music and conducting a children's orchestra. When he compared his family's poverty in Paris with the American Dream this job offer represented, he quickly accepted.

Yo-Yo loved living in America. He studied happily and played the cello as much as he could. He began taking lessons from Janos Scholz, a well-known cellist, and even played once for renowned musician Pablo Casals, who suggested Yo-Yo participate in a fund-raiser that was coming up in Washington, DC.

The event would be a symphony conducted by Leonard Bernstein, and it would also be aired on the television special *An American Pageant of the Arts*. President John F. Kennedy had set it up in order to raise money for the national cultural center that was to be built in the nation's capital. It was Yo-Yo's first opportunity to play a cello solo with a symphony, and he was phenomenal. The nation loved him! Before long, he was invited to play on *The Tonight Show*.

By the time Yo-Yo was nine, his father was working at the French school Ecole Française, and Yo-Yo went to school there. When the parents and teachers decided to organize a fund-raiser concert for the school, they went all out and reserved Carnegie Hall, one of America's most famous concert halls. Some of the parents, like Isaac Stern, were famous musicians themselves, so they performed first. Then Yo-Yo's father directed the student orchestra, and finally, Yo-Yo and his sister played Sammartini's *G Major Cello Sonata*. A *New York Times* reporter sat in the audience and later wrote, "This is no children's

> In Chinese, YO means "friend" and MA means "horse," so Yo Ma is "friendly horse." Yo-Yo's parents thought just one yo didn't sound very musical, though, so they added another: Yo-Yo Ma.

piece, nor did they play like children. The performance had assurance, poise, and a full measure of delicate musicality."

As Yo-Yo approached adolescence, he became more and more aware of the cultural differences between his strict, formal Chinese background and the informal, outspoken American ways. While he was expected to be silent at home, his teachers wanted him to speak up. His new cello teacher at the Julliard School, Leonard Rose, was just like his other teachers, and Yo-Yo was so intimidated, he initially tried to hide behind his cello. As time went on, though, Yo-Yo became more comfortable in all of these settings, and his musical talent continued to flourish.

At age fifteen, Yo-Yo was back at Carnegie Hall for his debut professional recital. Since then, he has performed professionally at famous concert halls around the world. Now he has been an exclusive Sony Classical artist for thirty years, releasing seventy-five albums in the process. He's even won fifteen Grammy Awards!

But Yo-Yo never forgets the teachers he's had along the way and the many children of the world who are as hungry for music teachers as he was. Every time he does a tour, he also sets up educational programs in the cities he's visiting. He teaches master classes for advanced musicians and workshops for kids just getting started. He also helped launch Family Concerts at Carnegie Hall, a low-cost concert series that helps parents introduce their children to music from around the world.

HOW WILL YOU ROCK THE WORLD?

I plan to rock the world's socks off. I want to do this with the power of medicine. Hopefully I will be a pediatrician. I will be putting a sense of security in the minds of parents. I will take care of their children because children are the future. They are the world. Eventually when we pass away, the only thing we leave behind is our bloodline. Since I want to be a pediatrician, I would ensure the safety of the future and its people.

BOBBY LAZZARA ☼ AGE 14

Bill Gates

1955– ❈ SOFTWARE DEVELOPER ❈ UNITED STATES

Software creation is . . . a mix of artistry and science.

—BILL GATES

Sixteen-year-old Bill looked up from the Traf-O-Data—a machine he and his friend Paul invented to solve traffic problems. The city official sat on the couch in the Gates' living room and cleared his throat, waiting impatiently for Bill's demonstration to start. Bill fed a piece of tape with instructions into the Traf-O-Data, which was designed to analyze cumbersome traffic data in a matter of minutes. The machine whirred a few times, then nothing.

"Tell him, Mom. Tell him it *really* works!"

"I don't have time for this, kid," the man said in frustration, getting up to leave. "Try me again when you're out of high school."

Little did the city official know that this frustrated boy standing before him would become one of the youngest billionaires in US history. But Bill knew. He had already told many of his friends that he would be a millionaire by age twenty-five. Even at sixteen, he had already founded his own computer company and invented the Traf-O-Data machine.

William Henry Gates III (or Trey, as his family called him) was born in Seattle in 1955. His parents were strict and enforced several house rules: keep your room clean and no television on weeknights. Without television, Bill devoured countless books—especially science fiction. But no matter how much his parents bugged him, Bill's room was a disaster area. This messy look would later become one of his trademarks at Microsoft.

Computer bugs first got their name in 1945 when a research assistant found a moth in one of the first experimental computers.

The Gates family played lots of board games together, and Bill was extremely competitive. In fact, he was competitive in just about *everything*. When Bill's teacher assigned the class to write four to five pages, Bill wrote thirty. But his enthusiasm didn't help his grades much, so Bill's parents transferred him to a private school in the seventh grade. He struggled academically and socially during his first year at the new school. He was much smaller than other boys his age, and he had enormous feet—size 13—but eventually he made some friends, including Kent Evans. Bill and Kent both liked math and science, and read *Fortune* magazine together. "We were going to conquer the world," said Bill.

In 1985, Bill and Paul Allen donated $2.2 million to their old high school for a math and science center named after their friend Kent Evans.

After two years at the private school, Bill found his niche. That year the school bought a Teletype machine. At the time, the only computers in existence were huge mainframe computers that cost millions of dollars. The Teletype machine connected the school to a mainframe computer downtown, and the students were charged an hourly rate for their computer time. Bill hung out in the computer room constantly and soon learned the programming language BASIC (Beginner's All-purpose Symbolic Instruction Code) to communicate with the computer. He created his first computer program, a tic-tac-toe game, at thirteen! He then wrote other game programs: a lunar landing game and computer versions of his favorite board games, Risk and Monopoly.

Bill was addicted to the computer and soon met other computer nerds, including Paul Allen. By ninth grade, Bill's grades were vastly improved. "I came up with a new form of rebellion," he said. The computer offered an outlet for Bill's creative and mathematical mind but it also got him into trouble. Some of his programs were known to crash the entire mainframe. Bill and his friends often broke into the computer's security system to change their computer time so they would be charged less. When the hackers were eventually caught, Bill was almost expelled!

As his reputation for programming grew, Bill was often approached by teachers asking for computer help. The school wanted Bill and Kent to design a computer program to help with class scheduling. They even offered to pay them for it! But a week later, tragedy struck. Kent, who had gone mountain climbing, fell and died. Bill was devastated by his best friend's death; they had been inseparable since they had first met. For weeks Bill was stunned, incapable of doing anything at all. He eventually went back to work on the scheduling program, asking Paul Allen to help him finish.

Bill and Paul went on to create the Traf-O-Data machine. Even though Traf-O-Data didn't *always* work perfectly, it was a success. Cities all over the Northwest and Canada eventually used it to analyze traffic data and to reduce congestion on city streets. As the money began to flow in, Bill's business skills emerged. He hired his buddies and classmates to work for the company. From their invention, Bill and Paul earned

> Bill and his wife set up the Bill and Melinda Gates Foundation, which has made some of the largest charity donations in history. In 2010 they donated $10 billion for the development and distribution of vaccines to people in the world's poorest locations.

> As a break from work, Bill and his friends would sometimes sneak onto empty construction sites and have bulldozer races!

over $20,000 (which in 1970 was a serious chunk of change for a couple of teenagers!). They also helped design a computer program for the Bonneville Power Administration to control the power grid for the entire Northwest and a program for TRW, a defense contractor.

With his improved grades and high test scores, Bill won a National Merit Scholarship and was accepted at Harvard University, where he studied literature, social science, math, and chemistry. But his mind was always on computers. People thought Bill was crazy when he predicted that, one day, everyone would have *their own personal computer.*

Bill's prediction was on track when, in 1975, Ed Roberts invented the Altair. Although the Altair couldn't do much compared to today's computers (it had only 4K of memory and didn't even have a keyboard), it was the first true PC. A technical revolution had arrived—and Bill and Paul hoped to be a part of it. They formed a new company called Microsoft (an abbreviation for microcomputer software) and decided to build a BASIC software program for the Altair. For the next seven weeks, Bill and Paul worked day and night to create the program. Finally, they finished it—the *first* software program for a PC. Bill was just nineteen years old.

Orders began pouring in for their new computer software—the first year revenues were more than $100,000! By January of 1977, Bill dropped out of Harvard to run Microsoft full time. He and Paul hired some of their old computer pals from Lakeside to work for them. Known as the Microkids, this gang of computer programmers was anything but typical. Many customers were shocked to hear rock music playing as the long-haired Microkids created software in jeans and T-shirts, instead of the suits and ties typical of most businesses.

In 1981, Bill met with IBM to discuss the opportunity of a lifetime. IBM wanted Microsoft to develop an operating system for its new PC. Even though Bill was late for the meeting (he had to buy a tie first), he convinced IBM to go with Microsoft. IBM's new PC became a hit, and every IBM computer had Microsoft software, MS-DOS. At twenty-four, Bill had made the deal of the century! Other computer companies began making IBM clones (copies of IBM's PC), and they *all* used Microsoft software. By 1987, thirty-two-year-old Bill Gates was the youngest billionaire in the country.

Microsoft has been involved in the computer industry almost from the very beginning, and it's still a strong presence today. The company's most famous products include MS-DOS, Windows, Internet Explorer, Microsoft.NET, and the Microsoft Office Suite. Bill semiretired in 2008, scaling back his daily involvement as chairman of the company to part-time so he could focus on the philanthropic goals of the Bill and Melinda Gates Foundation. Through the foundation, Bill and Melinda hope to "fund innovative ideas that could help remove ... barriers: new techniques to help farmers in developing countries grow more food and earn more money; new tools

> Bill used some of his fortune to build his dream house. It has a theater, a dining room that seats 120 people, a trampoline room, a swimming pool, and parking space for his 20 sports cars.

to prevent and treat deadly diseases; new methods to help students and teachers in the classroom. ... We think an essential role of philanthropy is to make bets on promising solutions that governments and businesses can't afford to make."[11]

ROCK ON!

NATHANIEL STAFFORD

Nate Stafford was sickened by the fact that more than two hundred million cases of malaria occur every year. And he loved to hike. So in 2010 he put the two pieces together and decided to hike a hundred miles in nine days as a fund-raiser to send one thousand nets to people in Africa. The nets help prevent them from being bitten by malaria-carrying mosquitoes. The hike was a huge success, and several local newspapers and news channels covered Nate's mission. But the most important thing to Nate is that he got to help people stay healthy. You can donate nets, too, at *nothingbutnets.net.*

Steve Jobs

1955–2011 ❀ COMPUTER PROGRAMMER AND INVENTOR
UNITED STATES

More than anyone else of his time, [Steve Jobs] made products that were completely innovative, combining the power of poetry and processors.

—WALTER ISAACSON, BIOGRAPHER

S teve felt a tingling sensation come over his body as he stared at the object in front of him. The sleek plastic panels swept around the corners of the machine, the keyboard featured four sets of keys, and the screen spanned just a few inches. And it *only* weighed about forty pounds—the Hewlett-Packard 9100A was by far the smallest computer Steve had ever seen! "It was a beauty of a thing," he said. "I fell in love with it."

That was back before Steve Jobs became one of the most famous computer programmers in the world. Back then, Steve was just a thirteen-year-old kid in the Hewlett-Packard Explorers Club, which taught kids to be excited about electronics. "They would get an engineer from one of the labs to come and talk about what he was working on," Steve said about the Explorers Club. That particular night, Steve had asked a laser engineer to show him one of the labs, and there it was: the 9100A, the first desktop computer. Before then, computers were so big, they took up entire rooms. By the time Steve died in 2011, computers were so small, they fit in a coat pocket.

Steve Jobs was born in San Francisco, California, to Joanne Schieble, a graduate student at the University of Wisconsin. But Joanne was in a tough situation. She loved Steve's father, Abdulfattah "John" Jandali, but her father was a strict Catholic, and when she got pregnant, he threatened to cut her out of the family if she married Abdulfattah, a Muslim. So Joanne decided not to marry Adbdulfattah, and she went to San Francisco to have her baby, where she would put him up for adoption. She left it up to the agency to choose the adoptive family, but she was adamant that the parents be college graduates. With that demand, the adoption agency selected a family, and everyone waited anxiously for the birth.

> In 1970, 175,000 children were adopted in America, setting a record that still holds today.
>
> ⁓⁓⁓

But when Steve was born, the family decided they would rather have a daughter than a son. Steve was without a family! The agency quickly chose another husband and wife—a mechanic and a bookkeeper, neither of whom had a college degree—and sent Steve home with them. When Joanne found out, she was furious, but Steve was already settling in to his new home. What could she do? She finally gave up the fight, but she did make Paul and Clara Jobs—Steve's new parents—sign a pledge to save money to send Steve to college.

Steve's parents took this oath to support his education seriously. Although they did not make a lot of money, they saved every bit they could and sent him to the best schools they could afford. When Steve was in middle school, his parents even sold their house to buy one they could barely afford in a nicer neighborhood—that way Steve could attend the better school. During much of Steve's childhood, his dad would buy cars for cheap, fix them up, and then sell them for more. "My college fund came from my dad paying $50 for a . . . beat-up car that didn't run, working on it for a few weeks, and selling it for $250." Steve would later show that same entrepreneurial spirit when he would buy used circuit boards at a flea market and sell them to the local electronics store to make a profit.

Steve didn't take his education quite as seriously as his parents or his birth mother, though. He felt bored in class and often focused his attention on pranking his classmates and teachers. One of these jokes involved making Bring Your Pet to School Day posters to hang all over the school. This led to a chaotic—but probably humorous—day of dogs chasing cats through the halls. Steve's parents and teachers agreed that he needed a more challenging environment to keep him focused on learning. He skipped fifth grade and went straight to middle school.

At that time, the technology industry in California was booming. Hewlett-Packard, the NASA Ames Research Center, and the Lockheed Missiles and Space Division were just a few of the companies producing new electronics all the time, and they were on all sides of the Jobs family. When their neighbor Larry Lang, an engineer for Hewlett-Packard, noticed Steve's aptitude for electronics and invited him to HP's Explorers Club, Steve jumped at the chance.

For one of his Explorers Club projects, fifteen-year-old Steve decided to build a frequency counter, a device that measures electronic signals. He didn't have all the parts he needed, though. But instead of going to the nearest electronics store to buy them, he called up the CEO of Hewlett-Packard, Bill Hewlett himself. Some might say Steve Jobs was a little out of the ordinary—and gutsy. Surprisingly, Bill was pleased to hear from the young electronics enthusiast and talked with him for twenty

> In the 1970s, the microprocessor, used in computers, was hugely in demand. Because silicon is used in making microprocessors and because most of them were manufactured in the Santa Clara Valley, this region of California was quickly nicknamed Silicon Valley.

minutes. He agreed to get the parts for Steve, and then he offered Steve a job at Hewlett-Packard!

Steve worked the HP assembly line building frequency counters, but he soon learned that he would rather hang out with the engineers than with the other assembly line workers. Every morning at ten, the engineers had coffee and doughnuts one floor above the assembly line, so Steve went upstairs and had a doughnut with a roomful of engineers. It didn't matter that none of the other assembly line workers went up there; Steve bent social norms when he thought it was the best thing to do.

When Steve was a junior in high school, he met Steve Wozniak, who was a few years older and shared interests in building electronics and playing pranks. One prank they played combined both these interests. They built a device that emitted television signals so that when they were watching TV with a group of people, they could control how fuzzy or clear the picture came in on the screen. When the picture got fuzzy, someone would get up to adjust the antenna, and just then, Steve and Steve would make the picture seem clear. When the person would sit back down, they'd adjust the signal again so their friends were jumping up and down all night long!

The two Steves became great friends. And they would go on to develop one of the most successful technology companies in the world: Apple.

After high school, Steve didn't really want to go to college. But his parents had been saving his whole life to fulfill their promise to his birth mother. Steve finally decided to go to Reed College in Portland, Oregon. He'd heard there were a lot of forward thinkers there,

> Have you ever typed on a typewriter? The letters are all the same size, and you don't have any options for how they look. In the 1980s, computer programmers started designing new fonts, like Times New Roman and Torino. You could also stylize the fonts—make them almost as big as you wanted and even italicize or bold them. Now thousands of fonts are available, each with its own artistic appeal.

and he imagined being able to take whatever classes he was interested in, whenever he felt like it. To his surprise, even such a progressive school had strict academic requirements, and he did not like the classes the school had enrolled him in.

Fortunately, the dean (like the principal) at the college noticed Steve's potential and decided to allow a special circumstance: Steve could audit classes. Auditing college courses means taking classes for a discount rate, but he wouldn't get credit toward an associate's or bachelor's degree. That was fine with Steve. He didn't even know what he wanted to do professionally yet—how could he pick what he wanted his degree to be in?

One of the classes Steve audited was calligraphy, the art of drawing fancy letters for writing. It may not seem like calligraphy has anything to do with computers, but this actually helped Steve a lot when he was working at Apple. In calligraphy class, he learned about letter shapes, which helped him design computer fonts!

When Steve was nineteen, he moved back to California where he took a job at Atari, one of the first video game companies, and started brainstorming with Steve Wozniak again. Just two years later, the two Steves decided to go into business. The Apple I was released in 1976, and they made $774,000 from its sales. Then the Apple II made them $139 million and attracted plenty of public attention. The next logical step was to let the public buy stock in the company, but that meant the company was owned by the public now, not by Steve and Steve anymore.

In the 1980s, Apple suffered from low sales and less than ideal products. There was a lot of tension between Steve Jobs and the board of directors, so Steve left Apple in 1985. He went on to create NeXT, Inc. and to buy an animation studio that would boom in the '90s and 2000s as Pixar Animation Studios.

In 1997, after twelve years away, Steve returned to Apple with a new vision. He wanted to implement a new management team, adjust stock

Pixar was started by George Lucas, of STAR WARS fame. Steve Jobs bought it in 1986 for $10 million, and Disney bought it in 2006 for $7.4 billion. What an investment!

options, and develop new products that would put Apple back at the front of the electronics world. And it worked. The iMac, iPod, iPhone, and iPad have earned Apple billions of dollars, and Apple has been rated number one in America's Most Admired Companies.

In 2003, Steve was diagnosed with pancreatic cancer. He underwent surgery for the tumor, but by 2011, the cancer had spread to his bones. He was fifty-six years old when he died.

HOW WILL YOU ROCK THE WORLD?

I will rock the world by being an engineer that designs computers, because I know a lot about computers and have experienced putting a computer together with my dad. I'm also very good at math and figuring things out—like problem solving and coming up with creative solutions.

JEFFREY ALLEN HASKELL ⚛ AGE 11

CameRON CRowe

1957– ✦ JOURNALIST AND MOVIE DIRECTOR ✦ UNITED STATES

Love the job. Be the job.

—CAMERON CROWE

The fifteen-year-old kid shifted his weight from foot to foot, his breath forming puffs of mist in the air. He had been waiting for twenty minutes in the freezing cold for the band to arrive at the backstage door. He clutched a small yellow pad and his favorite pen. Finally, a big silver bus pulled up, and four guys in big furry coats and sunglasses stepped off. As they pushed past the crowd of excited fans, he stuck out his pad of paper toward one of the band members.

"Excuse me," he said. "I'm here to—" But the rocker interrupted him by snatching his pad and scribbling a flamboyant signature across the entire page. The kid looked down at his pad, then back up at the backs of the band members as they disappeared through the backstage door.

"Wait! I'm here to interview you for *Rolling Stone Magazine*," he shouted, "not to get an autograph." His voice trailed off as the door slammed shut.

Cameron is married to a real-life rocker, Nancy Wilson of the band Heart.

—◆◆◆—

Cameron Crowe did eventually get his interview, but it took a lot of convincing for the security guard to let him in, and then even more convincing for the group to let a fifteen-year-old interview them. A bad review could break a band, and most rock stars were amazed to discover that a kid wielded such power over their careers. It was hard to believe that a teenager was writing for premier rock magazine *Rolling Stone*. But it was true, and Cameron would soon become well-known, not only as a gifted writer but also as a trustworthy friend to the bands.

Amazingly, this rock 'n' roll scribe was forbidden to listen to that kind of music when he was a kid. His mother, a college professor, believed it was "filth disguised as candy." It was Cameron's sister who first introduced him to rock 'n' roll. When she left for college, she gave him all her forbidden records. Crowe locked himself in his room for hours, secretly poring over such gems as *Led Zeppelin II*, *Deep Purple*, and the Beach Boys' *Pet Sounds*.

Cameron quickly fell in love with rock music and searched out anything having to do with it. In the early 1970s, you had to be eighteen to buy rock magazines like *Creem* or *Rolling Stone*, but Cameron made friends with the man at the shop where they were sold, and he let Cameron look at them while hanging out in the shop.

Patrick Fugit, the boy who played Cameron's character in the movie ALMOST FAMOUS, had never acted before that movie.

—◆◆◆—

Cameron's fate as an extraordinary teen was sealed when his sister took him to a meeting for the local alternative paper, the *San Diego Door*. At the meeting, he talked to lots of cool people who encouraged him to get into journalism. But when the fourteen-year-old asked if he could write music reviews for the journal, the staff was unsure. They believed rock and roll was a money-making scam. But eventually they gave in and put Cameron in touch with Lester Bangs, a former *Creem* and *Rolling Stone* writer. Cameron was so excited, he could barely stand it; Bangs was a professional rock journalist!

Bangs gave Cameron lots of advice, and the next year he was ready to submit his own writing to *Rolling Stone*. He lied about his age, telling them he was eighteen. The editor there was truly impressed with Cameron's writing and hired him to interview Richie Furay of the band Poco (other band members included such greats as Neil Young and Stephen Stills, who would later form Crosby, Stills, Nash and Young). Cameron did such a great job with the interview that in 1973 *Rolling Stone* made him a permanent staff writer. He was just sixteen years old.

Cameron's first traveling assignment was a tour with the Allman Brothers. His mother freaked out a bit, but then she realized it was Cameron's opportunity of a lifetime. The band was notorious for giving short and guarded interviews, and they didn't trust *Rolling Stone*, which had published some harsh reviews of their music. But Cameron had a strange effect on rock stars; he was so young and sincere that bands opened up to him, telling him all sorts of secrets they would never tell other reporters.

The first film Cameron directed was one he also wrote. 1989's SAY ANYTHING starred John Cusack and was about a dorky outsider who falls for a brainy, popular girl.

In his years as a journalist, Cameron interviewed such rock legends as Led Zeppelin, Yes, The Who, David Bowie, Elton John, Peter Frampton, Lynyrd Skynyrd, and most everyone else you hear on classic rock stations. Cameron made a name for himself writing catchy, true-to-life articles and for never betraying a band's trust. And they all loved him for it. Many bands refused to be interviewed by anyone else because Cameron was the only writer they liked.

By 1979, the twenty-two-year-old writer had big plans for a book. Although Cameron never finished high school, he decided to go undercover in a southern California high school in order to get inside the mind of the American teen. He enrolled in classes, pretending to be a senior named Dave Cameron, and immediately blended right in. No one suspected a thing. He hung out with his new friends after school and at

Cameron has since written other books, including CONVERSATIONS WITH WILDER and LET IT BLURT: THE LIFE AND TIMES OF LESTER BANGS, AMERICA'S GREATEST ROCK CRITIC.

the mall; he went to their parties and to football games. When something interesting happened, he would sneak off to a bathroom and whisper into a tape recorder. Finally, after a year of spying, Cameron finished the book, which he called *Fast Times at Ridgemont High*.

When Universal Studios released a movie based on the book in 1982, it made some waves. *Fast Times at Ridgemont High* showed what life was *really* like for teens—Cameron didn't hide the wild and crazy, and often painful, times he experienced at the high school—but many parents didn't want to see it . . . or believe it. Even with the controversy, the movie was a hit. It's still considered a cult classic and has been watched by thousands of kids and adults around the world.

Cameron went on to write and direct many more successful films, including *Singles*, *Jerry Maguire*, *Vanilla Sky*, *Elizabethtown*, *We Bought a Zoo*, and *Almost Famous*, the story of his own life as a teenage rock reporter. Cameron, now more than "almost famous," still writes and directs from his heart. His life was full of bold leaps: into journalism, then novels, then movies. And with each leap, Cameron showed the world that faith in yourself and a positive outlook can make anything possible.

ROCK ON!

KISHAN SHRIKANTH

Kishan Shrikanth doesn't let his age hold him back. At just nine years old, he became the youngest film director in history! His first movie, *C/o Footpath*, is about a slum boy in India who is adopted by a woman who wants to help him. With this little boost, he decides to make a change in his life. It won the Best Children's Film Award at the National Film Awards in India. At fourteen, Kishan was already at work on his second film, this time "about teenagers and the issues they face."

SheRmaN Alexie

1966– ◈ WRITER ◈ UNITED STATES

I write books for teenagers because I vividly remember what
it felt like to be a teen facing everyday and epic dangers. I don't
write to protect them. It's far too late for that. I write
to give them weapons—in the form of words and ideas—
that will help them fight their monsters.

—SHERMAN ALEXIE

Even though he was just a toddler, Sherman turned the crisp, white pages of the picture book and read the words on his own. This was the first new book he'd ever read—all the others had been around for generations, it seemed, and their pages were dirty and crinkled. But what was even more fascinating about this book was that it was about a little black boy. It was *The Snowy Day*, by Ezra Jack Keats, and as Sherman read each page about Peter exploring his city after the first snowfall of the year, Sherman felt that he had found a friend—someone with similar experiences—in this book.

Sherman was neither black nor in the city—he was American Indian and on a reservation—but for the first time, he was seeing a minority child in a book. He didn't have to imagine the kids in the illustrations having a skin color other than white, and this brought an overwhelming feeling of kinship. Sherman and Peter were more alike than they were different. As Sherman grew, he would remember the closeness he felt to Peter that first time he read *The Snowy Day*, and he would also write stories featuring characters his readers could relate to, though in a much different way.

Sherman Alexie was born in Spokane, Washington, on October 7, 1966, to parents from the Spokane and Coeur d'Alene Indian tribes. He was born with a condition called hydrocephalus, which is often called water on the brain. He had brain surgery when he was six months old, and although the surgery went well, doctors thought Sherman would be developmentally disabled his whole life. By the time he was three years old, though, Sherman had proved them all wrong—he had a high intelligence and was already reading!

Life on the reservation was not easy. Most of the residents were poor, and many struggled with alcoholism and other addictions. And, like many small towns, the rez was home to several bullies. This was especially frustrating for Sherman, who had seizures as a result of his hydrocephalus and was also extremely smart. He was an easy target.

While hydrocephalus has been called water on the brain, the liquid is actually cerebrospinal fluid. Everybody has this fluid in their brain, but if people have too much, it can damage the tissue in the brain. If surgery is completed successfully and early enough, the damage is only temporary.

Sherman started attending school in the nearest town, Reardon. He was the only Indian there, and he often felt challenged in his identity. His neighbors on the reservation felt he was shedding his Indian identity to go to the all-white school, but he didn't fit in with his classmates either. This experience became the inspiration for one of Sherman's later books, *The Absolutely True Diary of a Part-Time Indian*. Young adults from all backgrounds can relate to the main character's experiences in trying to figure out his identity.

While Sherman has loved to read since he was very small, he waited until college to start to write. First, it was a big deal that Sherman was going to college. Very few Indians went to college at that time, and nobody from his reservation had ever graduated from college. But his family supported him—even his brothers and sisters gave him money to help pay for tuition and books.

> Sherman was a star basketball player at his high school. He played on the varsity team, and he still loves the sport. In fact, basketball is hugely popular on the Spokane reservation.
>
> ~mm~

Sherman first wanted to study medicine, but that changed when he attended a poetry writing workshop at Washington State University. Then a professor gave him a book that included stories by American Indians Leslie Silko and James Welch. "It was the first time I'd seen anything creative by an Indian," Sherman said in an interview. "Everything else was archaic, loincloth literature. But they combined the day-to-day desperation of being Indian with the magic of being alive, in poems about powwows, broken-down cars, the food we eat, basketball. It was a revelation."[12]

By the time Sherman was twenty-five, he was hooked on writing—and readers were hooked on him. He was awarded a Washington State Arts Commission Fellowship, and his first poetry book, *The Business of Fancydancing*, was published that year too. The next year he received a National Endowment for the Arts Poetry Fellowship, one of the highest honors a poet can receive. His first short story collection, *The Lone Ranger and Tonto Fistfight in Heaven*, won a PEN/Hemingway Award for Best First Book of Fiction in 1993.

"This Is What It Means to Say Phoenix, Arizona" is a story from this collection that is about a young man named Victor, who has grown up without knowing his father. When he learns of his father's death, he plans a trip to Phoenix to pick up the truck his father left him. Along the way, he learns much about himself, his family, and the roles of sons and friends. This story is the basis for the movie *Smoke Signals*, which came out in 1998 and won the Sundance Festival Audience Award and the Filmmakers Trophy.

In his first novel, *Reservation Blues*, Sherman tells the story of an Indian band that plays the blues. Sherman has gone on to write many more books in each of these categories, including:

Poetry: *First Indian on the Moon, Water Flowing Home, The Man Who Loves Salmon*

Short Stories: *The Toughest Indian in the World, Ten Little Indians, War Dances*

Novels: *Flight, The Absolutely True Story of a Part-Time Indian, Indian Killer*

To say Sherman is a success would be an understatement. He helps readers learn the challenges that much of the Indian community experiences—such as racism and lack of opportunity—and to overcome their own battles with identity and purpose. He hopes that kids today relate to the authenticity of his characters and also feel inspired by his transcendence of the poverty and addiction he grew up with.

And he's still an avid reader. Instead of using his wealth to buy fancy cars and mansions, Sherman says he gauges his wealth by a different standard: "When I'm in a store and there's a book I want, I can always buy it. I never have to think about whether or not I can afford the book. I can buy a book a day, two books a day, three books a day, if I want. You talk about luxury, privilege? For me *that's* privilege."[13]

HOW WILL YOU ROCK THE WORLD?

I'm going to rock the world by becoming a children's book writer. I will write picture books, chapter books, and history books. I have a special book that I write poems in whenever I can. I've written a poem called "The Living Desert" and a story called "Kevin, the Duck." My poem "Ducky is Lucky" was published.

JURE ERLIC ☼ AGE 8

Will Smith

1968– ❖ ACTOR ❖ UNITED STATES

"Let's put it this way," says one studio head, "there's Will Smith, and then there are the mortals."

—NEWSWEEK

It was a neighborhood party, like so many others—Will had been performing at parties like this since he was just a kid. But there was something different about tonight. He could feel it.

He'd been emceeing with his friend DJ "Jazzy" Jeff, and they'd rocked the party—people loved Jeff's beats and Will's lyrics. Together, it seemed like they might really be able to go somewhere.

Whatever Will did, he knew, he was going to be big. Sure, he had a lot of charm and natural magnetism—that's why his high school teachers had nicknamed him Prince. But just a few years earlier, that natural charm hadn't kept his girlfriend from cheating on him. Ever since then, he'd been determined not just to be good, but to be the best at whatever he pursued.

Willard Christopher Smith Jr. was born in 1968 in Philadelphia. The son of a refrigeration engineer and an education professional (his mom worked for the School Board of Philadelphia), Will had plenty of school smarts, but he knew at an early age that he wanted to be an entertainer. He began performing rap music at parties around his neighborhood when he was just twelve, and this was how he began his collaboration with a childhood friend, DJ "Jazzy" Jeff Townes.

It was here that he caught the attention of Jeff's manager, James Lassiter, who would help to steer his career for the next twenty-two years. Eventually, James would establish Overbrook Entertainment, a production company named for the high school he and Will attended.

To his mom, education was everything—she even wanted him to apply to MIT. His SAT scores were pretty high, and he probably had what it took to get into MIT as a full-time college student. But Will wanted to be a rapper, a performer, and an entertainer. And since that was the career he had chosen, there was no way around it: he was going to be the best.

While Will's mother emphasized the importance of college, she agreed to let him take a year off to pursue music—if it didn't pan out, the deal was that he would focus on higher education. Will had had his first hit single with Jeff just a month shy of graduating high school under the stage name The Fresh Prince. The next year, 1987, he and Jeff came out with their first album, *Rock the House*, and went on tour with rap superstars Run DMC. It was here that Will got a taste of the big time and cemented his desire to reach as many people as possible with his art.

By the time their 1988 album *He's the DJ, I'm the Rapper* had gone multiplatinum and won the pair the first Grammy ever awarded to a

Will Smith and Jada Pinkett Smith, both actors, have two children—Jaden Christopher Syre Smith and Willow Camille Reign Smith—who have also chosen to pursue performing careers. Jaden has been nominated for three acting awards, and Willow's song "Whip My Hair" peaked at #11 on the BILLBOARD Hot 100 in 2010.

hip-hop album—and Will had bought his mom a 300E Mercedes—college was no longer an issue. It was clear where Will was headed: straight to the big time.

Will had the opportunity to move to Los Angeles in 1991, at the age of twenty-one, to star in *The Fresh Prince of Bel-Air*. This television series about a likable urban kid who'd come to live with wealthy relatives would run for nearly six years and make him a household name. Will told James at the time that if they were headed to Hollywood, they should have a goal. And his ambitions were simple: he wanted to be the biggest movie star in the world.

There were people who might have chalked that up to Will's youth, but James took him seriously. And so they began to study box office information on new movies and ticket sales, looking for trends. What was it, exactly, that made a blockbuster? Which movies grossed the most money?

They observed that, of the top ten movies of all time, ten had special effects or animation, nine had those two characteristics plus creatures, and eight had all three of those with a love story thrown in too. This was the information that would lead to them making *Independence Day* in 1996, which grossed $90 million in box office sales in its opening weekend.

> Will Smith's first nomination was for playing the legendary boxer Muhammad Ali in the movie ALI, in 2001.

Will's transition from television to film in the mid-1990s wasn't easy, though. Directors thought he was just a rapper (he and DJ Jazzy Jeff had won their second Grammy in 1991) and that his acting career was just a fluke—but Will got his break as a serious actor in the 1993 drama *Six Degrees of Separation*, in which he played a slick, young con man claiming to be Sidney Poitier's son. This performance turned a few heads, and Will's over-the-top 1995 action film *Bad Boys* sealed the deal: The Fresh Prince was box-office gold in the making.

Since then, Will has consistently delivered box-office hits, carefully selecting his scripts and roles for their global appeal. His recent films have grossed as much or more overseas than they have in the United States.

Action-oriented *Independence Day*; *Men in Black I & II*; *Wild Wild West*; *I, Robot* (which he also helped to produce); *I Am Legend*; and *Hancock* were all blockbusters, but Will has also seen success in the romantic comedy *Hitch* and the drama *The Pursuit of Happyness*, for which he received his second Oscar nomination.

Will is the only actor in history to have eight consecutive films gross over $100 million in the domestic box office, as well as the only actor to have eight consecutive films in which he starred that opened at the number one spot. Fourteen of the nineteen fiction films he has acted in have accumulated worldwide gross earnings of over $100 million, and four of them took in over $500 million from the global box office.

He has been nominated for four Golden Globe Awards, two Academy Awards, and has won two Grammy Awards. He has also produced, or helped to produce, numerous films.

In 2007, *Newsweek* named Will the most powerful actor in Hollywood. His handprints have been immortalized in the sidewalk outside Grauman's Chinese Theatre on Hollywood Boulevard in Los Angeles, alongside the handprints of many Hollywood icons before him.

ROCK ON!

JADEN SMITH

Jaden Smith was introduced to acting early—his parents are the famous Will Smith and Jada Pinkett Smith! But that doesn't mean he doesn't work hard. When his father was reading the script for the movie *The Pursuit of Happyness*, Jaden was interested in acting in it too. Will told his son he'd have to audition, just like all the other kids, so Jaden did. The producers loved him and immediately cast him. Since then, he's acted in *The Day the Earth Stood Still* and *The Karate Kid*.

Tony Hawk

1968– ❀ ATHLETE ❀ UNITED STATES

*The most important message, I think, is to believe in yourself,
you know, and go after whatever goals or aspirations you have
with confidence.*

—TONY HAWK

Eleven-year-old Tony ollied (bounced his skateboard) off the top of the ramp, then turned himself around 360 degrees. For a moment he was weightless. The board floated somewhere beneath him as he twisted in the air. Suddenly, Tony planted his feet back on the board and slammed it into the cement surface with a loud, satisfying *thrrack*. Just like that, he was at the other end of the ramp flipping himself in the air again like some strange, skinny dolphin.

Nearby, two boys laughed at some inside joke as they slowly rolled around on their skateboards. They were only Duane Peters and Steve Alba, two of the best pro skaters around! They sported an extreme punk look, and Tony wanted them to like him more than anything in the world. He skated over and started laughing with them, hoping they might just think he was in on their joke. But they weren't laughing anymore. Instead, they raised their eyebrows, as if to say, "Who's the twerp?" Duane spit, just missing Tony's shoes. "This is punk rock kid."

Steve doubled over laughing. Then Duane started laughing too. Tony was obviously not *in* on the joke. He *was* the joke. He picked up his board and walked slowly out of the park. Tony knew then that he still had a lot to learn about skating if he was going to be better than those guys. He vowed he would become the best skater in the world, just so he wouldn't have to take that kind of attitude from anyone. And that's just what he did.

Tony was such an odd child that his parents had him psychologically tested. The results? He wasn't odd; he was gifted. Tony has an IQ of 144—he's a certifiable genius!

But before he became the skateboarding champion of the world, Tony describes himself as a complete and total nightmare. "Instead of the terrible twos, I was the terrible youth," he said. "I was a hyper, rail-thin geek on a sugar buzz. . . . My mom summed it up best when she said 'challenging.'" Even as a toddler, he chucked toys at his elderly babysitter.

Tony was also unusually determined about achieving his goals. His first time at bat in a Little League game, he hit a single. He was stoked! But his next time up, he struck out. Tony immediately took off running across the outfield and disappeared into a ravine at the far end of the field. He stayed there until the game was over and his father bribed him out with an ice-cream sundae. Tony could be a little hard on himself.

In the late sixties and early seventies, skateboarding was actually called sidewalk surfing. Tony was just six when he first stepped onto an old blue fiberglass banana board at the prodding of his brother, Steve. He couldn't figure out how to turn, and he whined until his brother taught him how. He was no good at all, but as he says, "something had begun to itch." Tony's extreme energy and determination finally had an outlet.

By the fourth grade, the itch had gotten so bad that Tony formed a skating group with his neighborhood buddies and visited his first skate park, fittingly named Oasis. He begged for a membership, but instead, his dad built him a ramp of his own in their driveway.

The next year, after much convincing, Tony's mom finally let him skate at Oasis. The park swarmed with guys doing tricks, always looking like they were about to run into one another. Tony had to rent his safety equipment, which had often been worn by four guys in a single day. The elbow and kneepads were always soggy and stinky with other people's sweat. Padded up like a gladiator, he walked into the skating area. The tricks these guys were doing seemed impossible. How would he ever be able to do that stuff?

Well, it only took Tony a couple years to master all their tricks, plus invent a whole bunch of his own: the fakie to frontside rock and the frontside 540/rodeo flip (during which a skater does almost two whole rotations in the air). The reason Tony was so good? He was obsessed. He ate, slept, and breathed skateboarding, even though most people considered the sport uncool by the early eighties.

A group of professional skaters practiced at Oasis. Tony became friends with them and then joined their team, the Bones Brigade, just before his thirteenth birthday. Most skaters in the group were seventeen or eighteen years old, and twelve-year-old Tony was a bit intimidated to be skating with his idols. But the team manager, ex-world champion Stacy Peralta, had secretly been watching him for a year and recognized his "fierce determination." He had no worries about putting the kid on the team.

> Tony got his first sponsor, Dogtown Skateboards, when he was just 12 years old.

> Tony was so skinny when he first started skating that regular knee pads slid right off him. He had to use elbow pads instead, and even those slipped during his runs!

201

Tony has invented more than 80 tricks!

Tony started out skating as an amateur for the Bones Brigade, and his first competitions were disappointing. As he puts it, "I sucked for a while." He was barely over four feet tall and weighed just eighty pounds: "the walking noodle," as he called himself. But even though he wasn't the best skater on the team, Tony had his moments of glory—like when he picked up his favorite magazine, *Thrasher*, and saw a picture of himself doing a lien-to-tail on the cover. He had no idea anyone had even snapped the photo!

In 1982, at fourteen, Tony's dream finally came true; he became a professional skateboarder. But he still had a long way to go. He had a hard time getting air because he was so skinny and couldn't build the momentum he needed at the end of a half-pipe. But Tony was creative: to get more height, he would ollie into the air, bouncing his board off the end of the pipe. It worked, but some skaters got on his case for skating like a geek. It would take a few wins before anyone took Tony Hawk, the geeky fourteen-year-old pro, seriously.

While Tony was struggling up the ranks of the skateboarding world in the afternoons and on weekends, he was also struggling through the ranks of high school. Skateboarding was still uncool, and no one at school really knew (or cared) that Tony was a professional skateboarder. Tony was an easy target for the jocks to ridicule: he was scrawny and dressed in weird skater clothes. Back then the skateboarding style meant lots of skulls, baggy shorts, and duct-taped shoes. Everybody else was wearing skin-tight designer jeans!

Skating became Tony's only sanctuary. Over the next few years, Tony skated in more and more competitions.... He even began to win. In Tony's first professional win, he actually beat Duane Peters, the very same skater who'd spit at him years before. It was a sweet victory for Tony, the first of many.

By the age of sixteen, Tony was winning all the time. He was the undisputed skateboarding champion of the world, and his life got a whole lot better. He was no longer scrawny; at six feet, four inches tall, Tony towered over most kids at school. They finally left him alone.

Skateboarding was also starting to get popular, so Tony was earning quite a bit of money from all his sponsorships. By his senior year in high school Tony bought himself a house! Best of all, Tony felt he was skating up to his own standards—he was achieving his goals, landing tricks, and inventing new ones.

Tony dominated the skating world for years. By 1991 he had achieved so many of his goals and won so many contests that he felt it was time for a break. He retired and formed a skateboard company called Birdhouse. But Tony was never one to go quietly. He still had one more trick up his sleeve before he was through: the 900.

The 900 is probably the most difficult skateboarding trick known to man. It requires three full rotations in the air, and of course, a successful landing. Tony had been trying to do this trick since 1986, and he had one cracked rib and a crooked spinal cord to show for it. But in 1999, at the ripe old age of thirty-one (positively *ancient* in the skateboarding world), Tony landed the 900 at the X Games. The crowd roared as his buddies dog-piled on top of him—no skater on earth had ever landed it! It officially put Tony in skateboarding god status.

> By the time he was 23, Tony had competed in 103 pro contests. He won first place in 73 and second in 19—by far the best record in skateboarding history.

Since then, Tony has created more goals for himself and achieved every one. He's been in movies, ads, and video games, including Tony Hawk Pro Skater and Tony Hawk's Proving Ground. It is the closest most humans will ever get to landing a "frontside twist madonna."

In an effort to support other skateboarders, Tony created the Tony Hawk Foundation and donated more than $3 million to skate park projects around the United States. He is the subject of two books: *Hawk—Occupation: Skateboarder* and *How Did I Get Here? The Ascent of an Unlikely CEO*.

Thanks to Tony, skateboarding is more popular than ever and has paved the way for other alternative sports like snowboarding and surfing. Tony is a great role model for anyone who wants to push their limits.

ROCK ON!

NYJAH HUSTON

A true Southern California boy, Nyjah Huston loves to skate. He competed in the X Games when he was only eleven, and he still holds the record for the youngest X Games participant. When he was fifteen, he earned a street silver medal there, and he continues to compete, wowing judges and audiences alike, across the United States. Nyjah was even featured in Tony Hawk's video game Proving Ground in 2007.

HRithik Roshan

1974– ✤ ACTOR ✤ INDIA

Oh, I'm never satisfied. I'm always trying to aim for more, I'm a perfectionist. Honestly, sometimes when people praise me, I want to tell them to stop it. Call me modest or whatever, I'd rather let my work speak for me.

—HRITHIK ROSHAN

Six-year-old Hrithik stood nervously among all the adult actors. His grandfather had asked him to dance in the movie he was producing, *Aasha*, and although Hrithik was excited for it, what if he messed it up? *At least I don't have to say any lines*, Hrithik thought. Ever since his oral exam at school earlier that year, he stuttered every time he had to say something important. But this was just a dance, and Hrithik was good at that.

As the music neared his cue, Hrithik began tapping his foot with the beat. Then the cameras were on him, and his body flowed into the first steps of the dance. Before he knew it, the scene was over. Relief washed over him, and then adrenaline. Hrithik realized that he had just filmed his first part in a movie!

Hrithik's family wasn't new to the movie industry. His parents, Rakesh and Pinky, were both Bollywood actors in India, and his grandfather was a producer. Hrithik had spent the first six years of his life backstage at his family's movie sets. Now that he'd had a role in one too, he was hooked! Hrithik started dreaming of being a movie star. But his father wasn't sure that was such a good idea. After all, it's not easy to make it in the movie biz.

> India used to be called Bombay, so when the movie industry started to thrive there in the early 1900s—not long after Hollywood was gaining momentum—people put the B from Bombay on the front of the word HOLLYWOOD, and Bollywood was born.

Instead of signing Hrithik up for acting classes, Rakesh enrolled his son in speech therapy and told him to focus on school. Hrithik hated school, though. They were always scheduling him for oral exams, and every single time, he stuttered. The kids laughed at him. He got so frustrated that whenever a teacher set him up for an oral exam, Hrithik skipped school. But the speech therapy helped. The more Hrithik practiced the exercises his speech therapist assigned, the less he stuttered, and that made him happy. Someday, he'd show his classmates that he could talk just fine. Maybe he'd even prove it to them on the big screen!

Even though his parents didn't encourage Hrithik to pursue a career in acting, they were still happy to have him help with their movie projects. When he was twelve, he acted in a fight scene in *Bhagwaan Dada* with his father. He also acted as an assistant to his father, making sure he had everything he needed to do his best in front of the camera.

At his parents' insistence, Hrithik earned a bachelor's degree in communication at Sydneham College. They urged him to continue his studies at a foreign university, but Hrithik had another idea—he was going to secretly take acting classes! He was dedicated and studied every aspect of movie making—screenwriting, cinematography, and, of course, acting.

When he unveiled his new acting talent to his family that year, they were delighted. His father asked him to help with the screenplay for his newest movie, *Kaho Naa . . . Pyaar Hai* (Say . . . You Love Me), and then, to Hrithik's delight, invited his son to play the lead role! In the movie, Hrithik plays a young man named Rohit, who falls for Sonia. Together, they are surprisingly caught up in life-threatening scandals. After Rohit is murdered, Sonia meets Raj, who looks just like Rohit (and is also played by Hrithik). Raj and Sonia dodge more dangerous situations until they get to the bottom of the corruption.

> Hrithik said working for his dad on KAHO NAA . . . PYAAR HAI was like working for a completely different person. At home, Rakesh was relaxed and affectionate, but on the movie set, he demanded excellence. Hrithik attributes his dedication and professional work ethic to his father.

The movie was a huge hit. It made more money in India than any other movie that year, and it won eight Filmfare Awards. Hrithik won both Best Actor and Best Debut. At just twenty-six years old, he was a megastar. The dream he'd set when he was six years old had finally come true!

The media went berserk about Hrithik's role in *Kaho Naa . . . Pyaar Hai*. They called him a heartthrob and a stud, adored by young and old alike, and even went so far as to make his name an acronym: Handsomely Real Internationally Tested Hot Indian King. The country went so crazy over Hrithik, the phenomenon was called hrithikmania. Yet, with all this media attention, Hrithik stayed levelheaded:

I have seen people being lifted to the skies and then being pulled down, mercilessly, by the media, when it suits them. So I am neither elated by their pampering now; nor will I feel deflated when they bring me down, as they must. I hope to maintain a rational balance, without being swung around by the media. . . . The point I am making is that, even at this young age, I have seen it all and so know what is coming—I know I am no "phenomenon"! [14]

207

Hrithik decided that the dawn of his success was a good time to marry his longtime girlfriend, Sussanne Khan. They said their vows in December of 2000, and girls across the country were green with envy.

Hrithik wasted no time lining up future movie gigs. The public's expectations of Hrithik were incredibly high, though, and not all of his movies in the first few years were deemed successful. But Hrithik didn't let this get him down. He worked that much harder in future movies to ensure his directors and fans were happy.

In 2003 Hrithik worked with his father again on *Koi ... Mil Gaya* (I Found Someone): Bollywood's first science-fiction film. In it, Hrithik plays a developmentally disabled young man whose father used to communicate with aliens but died before he was born. When Hrithik's character grows up, he accidentally summons the aliens his father had contacted years before. The film was launched at the Jerusalem Film Festival and the Denmark NatFilm Festival, and then in Indian theaters. Once again, the crowds loved it. The movie won three National Film Awards and five Filmfare Awards, with Hrithik taking the trophies for Best Actor and Critics Award Best Performance.

> Hrithik's favorite Hollywood actor is Sylvester Stallone.

In 2011 Hrithik joined the international dance talent search *Just Dance*. He and his team held auditions across India, the United States, and the United Kingdom looking for dancers to share the stage with him. Dancers were slated to learn groovy moves from Hrithik and then to compete in front of judges for the title of ultimate dance champion.

Hrithik continues to be passionate about acting and movie making. Since 2000, he's played in more than two dozen films and continues to develop his art. "I am an actor first, a star after," he said. "I want to experiment with all kinds of characters. I certainly don't want to be stuck with just one kind of screen persona." And he still holds his status of heartthrob. When a wax statue replicating his chiseled muscles and intense gaze was unveiled in 2011, fans jumped at the chance to pose for photos with Hrithik—or at least a realistic replica.

HOW WILL YOU ROCK THE WORLD?

I would like to be a famous baseball player. I enjoy the game. Like when I'm up to bat sometimes, or when I play the catcher position and I try to throw someone out who is stealing a base, I get an adrenalin rush. My goal if I make it to the MLB is to change the way people look at the game of baseball. Kinda like Babe Ruth did. I would change the game by being one of the best players yet.

CHRISTIAN NEEDHAM AGE 13

The Black Eyed Peas

1995– ⚘ MUSICIANS ⚘ UNITED STATES AND PHILIPPINES

*If you go on to the Super Bowl stage—or any stage of that
magnitude—to win over fans, then you're performing for the wrong
reason. You need to be performing to make everybody feel good,
that's the only reason. It's entertainment, not business.*

—WILL.I.AM

William watched his best friend and bandmate, Allan, break it down on the dance floor. Allan had real talent, not just as a break-dancer, but as an emcee and drummer too. Ever since they'd met in their freshman year of high school, William knew the two of them were going to do something big together.

After William caught the eye of the famous Compton rapper, Eazy-E—who had his own label, Ruthless Records—he and Allan had gone on to form a band: Atban Klann. Atban stood for A Tribe Beyond A Nation, and for the last few years, they'd been rocking house parties like this and other events all over Southern California. They had the beats, the lyrics, the moves—and now, finally, a debut album, *Grass Roots*, coming out on Eazy-E's label.

Even as Allan went through the moves, though, he seemed focused somewhere far off, preoccupied. William knew why: not long ago, Eazy-E had died, and now it was becoming clear that their big debut album was never going to be released.

But as William picked up the microphone that night and flowed through the lyrics of the song they'd rehearsed so many times, he knew he was good. He knew Allan was good too. Deep down, he still believed they had what it took. Maybe they should change the name of the band, start fresh. There was that kid Jaime—maybe he should be in the band. And Dante said he knew an amazing female vocalist.

Everyone at the party was moving, heads nodding to the beat. What would it be like to have people all over the world tuned in to their music? William decided, then and there, he was going to talk to Allan about forming a new band. They couldn't let this setback get them down. He and Allan, they had big things to do.

After Eazy-E died in 1995, Atban Klann reformed and changed their name—first to the Black Eyed Pods, and then the Black Eyed Peas. The group originally consisted of rapper, multi-instrumentalist and producer will.i.am (William James Adams Jr.) and rappers apl.de.ap (Allan Pineda Lindo Jr.) and Dante Santiago. Before long, Dante was replaced with Taboo (Jaime Luis Gómez), and the band added vocalist Kim Hill, producing two albums, *Behind the Front* and *Bridging the Gap*.

> Rapper, musician, and producer will.i.am of the Black Eyed Peas also works as an electronic music DJ under his other stage-name, Zuper Blahq. While Zuper Blahq specializes in the electronic music genre known as electro, will.i.am admits that he and apl.de.ap were also big fans of house music in their youth. He told the LOS ANGELES TIMES, "Black Eyed Peas, before we were Black Eyed Peas, we were what you called 'house dancers.' We used to dance house."

William James Adams Jr.—a.k.a., will.i.am—was born in 1975 in Inglewood, California. He was raised in the projects of East Los Angeles with his siblings—two biological, and four adopted. His mom encouraged him to be different from other kids in his neighborhood, sending him to Palisades Charter High School in a wealthy area to challenge him. Here, he met future Black Eyed Peas bandmate Allan Pineda Lindo Jr., who became his best friend.

At sixteen, William was discovered by Compton rapper Eazy-E and came out with a song on a compilation from Ruthless Records under the name Will 1X. He and Allan then went on to form the Black Eyed Peas, which catapulted them into superstardom.

As a producer and an artist, will.i.am went on to work with a virtual Who's Who of pop, including Michael Jackson, Britney Spears, U2, Rihanna, Usher, Justin Timberlake, Nicki Minaj, Cheryl Cole, Mariah Carey, Whitney Houston, and Carlos Santana.

will.i.am has also acted or voice acted in a number of films, including *X-Men Origins: Wolverine*, a prequel to the X-Men series. If all that weren't enough, he also has his own line of clothing and currently serves as a creative director for software giant Intel, where he contributes music and helps to develop devices like laptops, smartphones, and tablets.

Allan Pineda Lindo Jr.—a.k.a., apl.de.ap—was born in 1974 in Angeles City, in the Philippines. His Filipino mom had a tough time raising him and his six younger siblings alone, but she got some assistance from Pearl S. Buck International, a foundation that arranged sponsorship for Allan through its dollar-a-day program.

When Allan was eleven, his American sponsor, Joe Hudgens, helped him come to the United States to treat an eye problem known as nystagmus (to this day, Allan is legally blind in both eyes). Allan told Joe he wanted to come to live in the United States, and three years later, in 1998, Joe officially adopted him.

Allan became friends with will.i.am in high school, and the two of them formed a band and break-dancing crew called Tribal Nation that performed regularly at Southern California parties and events. Later, they went on to form the Black Eyed Peas.

Allan's Filipino roots show through in a number of the band's songs, including "The Apl Song" on *Elephunk*, which contains lyrics in the

Tagalog language. As a successful performer with global reach, Allan also started the Apl Foundation, which gives back to communities and children within the Philippines and throughout Asia.

Jaime Luis Gómez—a.k.a., Taboo—was born in 1975 in Los Angeles. He joined the Black Eyed Peas in 1995 and is known for his martial-arts-inspired dance moves. (He is a practitioner of the style known as Jeet Kune Do, founded by Bruce Lee.) In addition to his role as a rapper and keyboardist with the band, he has also acted in a number of films, including *Dirty* with Wyclef Jean, and *Street Fighter: The Legend of Chun-Li*, where he got to show off his martial arts skills.

Jaime has collaborated musically with numerous Latin American performing artists, including George Pajon Jr. and Andy Vargas. He also performed in the Obama song "Yes We Can" (*Si Se Puede*), and coauthored a book with Steve Dennis, *Fallin' Up: My Story*, which was released in 2011.

Then, in 2002, former member Dante introduced the band to Fergie (Stacy Ferguson). The Black Eyed Peas went on to make *Elephunk* with her in 2003, working with former 'N Sync member Justin Timberlake on their breakout hit, "Where Is the Love?," which became the biggest selling single of the year in the United Kingdom. And the rest, as they say, is history.

The Black Eyed Peas' next album—*Monkey Business*, in 2005—opened at number two on the US *Billboard* 200 albums chart, selling over 295,000 copies in its first week. It was later certified triple platinum by the Recording Industry Association of America. *The E.N.D.*, in 2009, opened at number one on the *Billboard* 200, and though *The Beginning* was not their biggest album, it still debuted at number six on the *Billboard* charts.

> By 2011, the band had sold an estimated 56 million records worldwide.
>
> ~~~

The Black Eyed Peas were ranked twelfth on *Billboard*'s Artists of the Decade and seventh in the Hot 100 Artists of the Decade. They have won a total of three Grammy Awards and performed at the half-time show of SuperBowl XLV in 2011.

ROCK ON!

QUINN SULLIVAN

At twelve years old, guitarist Quinn Sullivan already had an album out and has received media attention from coast to coast. Quinn started playing guitar when he was three. When he was barely into elementary school, Ellen Degeneres featured him on her show, where she presented him with a brand-new Gibson ES-335, the same kind of guitar that Eric Clapton plays. Quinn was so surprised, he couldn't help but drop his jaw in shock! He's shared a stage with B. B. King and Buddy Guy, whose Grammy-nominated album *Skin Deep* features Quinn. Quinn's debut album *Cyclone* was released in 2011, and he continues to tour the United States playing the blues.

Mark Zuckerberg

1984– ◉ SOFTWARE DEVELOPER ◉ UNITED STATES

*My goal is to not have a job. Making cool things is just something
I love doing, and not having someone tell me what to do or a time
frame in which to do it is the luxury I am looking for in my life.*

—MARK ZUCKERBERG, AGE TWENTY

This is ridiculous," Mark heard his father, Edward, complain. Edward
ran a dental office out of the Zuckerberg family home, and everything was going quite well, except for the fact that his receptionist
had to yell—really HOLLER—down the hall, past the 160-gallon fish
tank, to let him know every time a patient arrived. It seemed the only
alternative would be to make her walk back to the dental exam rooms
every time, which would leave the reception area—and all the patient
records and business files stored there—vulnerable. No, that wouldn't
work either. "There's got to be a better way."

Twelve-year-old Mark didn't speak up right away, but his father's
need had sparked an idea. He headed upstairs to sort out the details.

Once settled into his room, Mark powered up his computer and began punching away at the keys. "If I set it up this way, maybe it will—" He paused and hit the backspace key a few times. "No, this will work better."

In no time, he had created a computer program he called Zucknet. It would allow the receptionist to send Dr. Zuckerberg an instant message on the computer to tell him when patients arrived. No more yelling needed!

> Mark says he works on a lot of small projects, coding one little idea here and there. Sometimes, they come together into one big product, like Facebook, but not always.

Pleased with his invention, Mark set the whole family—his parents and three siblings—up on Zucknet so they could chat with one another. Of course, between the siblings, chatting was less common than pranks were. One time Mark sent a message to his sister Donna while she was working on homework: the computer was going to explode in thirty seconds. "Maaaark!" she shrieked.

This was only one of Mark's many early computer programming adventures, though. His family was fairly well off and lived a comfortable life in Dobbs Ferry, New York. Like most kids, one of Mark's favorite things to do was invite his friends over. They would goof around and draw pictures, and then Mark would make a computer game out of the pictures.

Mark's parents recognized his talent, and when he was eleven, they hired a tutor to work with him once a week. That lasted a short while, until Mark enrolled in a night class on programming at Mercy College nearby. Mark was so young that the instructor didn't think he was a student, but the child of a student, and asked him to leave!

For high school, Mark attended Phillips Exeter Academy, where he studied classics, practiced fencing, and—of course—worked on computers. For his senior project, he and a friend developed a program called Synapse, which paid attention to a person's musical tastes and predicted songs the listener would want to play next. They put it up on the internet for free, where Slashdot.org found it and linked to it. Suddenly, companies like AOL, WinAmp, and Microsoft were contacting Mark and offering to buy the program. One offer was for $2 million! The friends decided to turn down all offers, though.

When Mark went to college at Harvard University, his program ideas kept coming. He developed one called CourseMatch to help students choose which classes to take based on the course popularity among other students. Then he launched Facemash, which put photos of two Harvard students next to each other and allowed people to choose which one was more attractive. The students thought it was hilarious, but the administration did not; the site was shut down within four hours.

That's when Cameron and Tyler Winklevoss, twins, and Divya Narendra approached Mark to help them with their project: HarvardConnection, later called ConnectU. It was late 2003, and Mark was a nineteen-year-old sophomore at Harvard. Cameron, Tyler, and Divya had been working on this project for two years, and they'd had the help of a few other people, but the programmers weren't able to finish the code. They needed Mark to help so they could launch the social network that would allow students at Harvard to create online groups of friends, post updates about what they were doing and how they were feeling, and upload pictures. They knew it was going to be a huge success.

Mark accepted the invitation and began work right away. There are different stories about what happened next, though. Some people think Mark stole Cameron, Tyler, and Divya's idea, while it's possible that the four just didn't work together very well and Mark was inspired to create his own social network. Either way, Mark never finished ConnectU. Instead, he launched thefacebook.com in early 2004.

Originally thefacebook.com was only for Harvard students. Within the first day of its launch, the site had over 1,200 members. A few months later, Mark opened the site up to other colleges in Boston, then to other Ivy League schools, then to colleges and universities across the country. In August 2005, Mark dropped *the* from the name, and the site was known as simply Facebook. The next month, high school-ers could sign up for a Facebook account too, and then in September 2006, the site was opened up to anyone with an email address. That's when the user numbers really soared. As of mid-2011, Facebook had

Facebook employs 1,700 people, and Mark expects only the best from his engineers. They embrace the term HACKER, which to them means "someone who builds something very quickly" (it can also mean "someone who cracks passcodes to obtain private information," but that's not the definition Mark focuses on). Sometimes they'll have Hackathons, when all the engineers, including Mark, stay up all night, working together to develop a new part of Facebook.

—⁊⁊⁊—

750 million users, more than half of whom checked the site on any given day. All together, people were spending more than 700 billion minutes on Facebook per month—if you were to line all those minutes up consecutively, they would equal 1.3 million years, or eighteen thousand lifetimes!

Not surprisingly, Mark has a Facebook page too. On it, he writes, "I'm trying to make the world a more open place by helping people connect and share." Through Facebook, he seems to be achieving that goal. Stories abound about people finding long-lost friends, adopted children finding birth parents, and medical patients finding organ donors, all through Facebook. It's even useful in politics—revolutionaries have used Facebook to organize civil rights revolts in countries like Yemen and Libya. Through applications, users can play games or tell their friends where they are at any given time. Companies can buy ads and target them to Facebook users who like things similar to their products or services. It seems there's hardly any social activity that one *can't* do on Facebook. In 2011 President Obama praised Mark for his innovation.

But the website is more than popular—it's also profitable. Until May 2012, the company was not publicly owned, meaning not just anyone could buy stock in it; it had investors. People basically gave money to Facebook so that the company could use it to do new things. Then, as the company grew and became worth more money, the investors could get their money—and then some—back. When the company went public, the value of Facebook was estimated at $104 billion,[16] and Mark

Zuckerberg was a rich twenty-eight-year-old, worth about $17.5 billion.[17]

In 2010 the biographical drama *The Social Network* was released. It's about Mark and his experience in building the Facebook empire. Even though it's a fictionalized account—Mark's never even seen it—the public went crazy over it. The movie won three Oscars and made over $96 million in theaters.

Many people are now asking, what's next? Mark's still only in his twenties, so he's got lots of time to write more code, develop more programs, and change the world in new ways.

ROCK ON!

John Collinson

Little Johnny Collinson was youngest person to climb Mount Rainier, at just four years old! He's been mountaineering his whole life, and when he was sixteen, he set the goal to be the youngest person to climb the Seven Summits—the highest peak on each of the seven continents. His mountain-climbing family and friends have supported him the whole way, and John has worked hard to obtain sponsors too. Between January 2009 and January 2010, John summited all seven peaks. Mission accomplished!

Shaun White

1986– ❧ ATHLETE ❧ UNITED STATES

White possesses insane skills and instantly recognizable looks. This amazing combination has made him one of the most recognizable sports figures of his time.

—TEAMUSA.ORG

At age six, Shaun knew a thing or two about skateboarding—he'd been hanging out with his older brother, Jesse, at the Encinitas YMCA. But now his brother had a new passion, and so did he: snowboarding.

Shaun loved the rush of the wind in his face as he bombarded the chilly slopes. He loved challenging himself to learn new tricks, to catch bigger and better air. But most of all, he loved speed—he couldn't go fast enough.

"Slow down!" his mom told him as he sped past her at the top of the slopes. She'd given him the ultimatum: he could only keep snowboarding if he rode switch. So what did Shaun do? He reached the top of the hill, turned around, and rode switch, all the way down. On his next run, he challenged himself to a new trick—backwards.

"What's that kid doing?" people wanted to know. Word got around about the crazy little red-haired speed demon on the slopes; later that year, Shaun got his first sponsorship, from Burton Snowboards.

> Switch means riding with your less dominant leg forward—a little like trying to write left-handed, if you're right-handed.

Born in 1986 in San Diego with a congenital heart condition, Shaun White went through two surgeries before the age of five. That didn't stop him, however, from skateboarding and snowboarding with his brother, Jesse—by the age of nine, Shaun not only had his first sponsorship but he'd also met skating legend Tony Hawk in Encinitas, California, at the local skate park. Tony took Shaun under his wing, helping him to go pro in skateboarding at seventeen—five years after he'd gone professional with snowboarding.

Shaun has always loved both sports, but to grow up snowboarding in Southern California takes some dedicated family support. Luckily, his close-knit clan helped him pursue his passion, even in the off season, driving him all the way from their home in Southern California to the ski parks at Mammoth Mountain in Central California and Mount Hood in Oregon so he could snowboard in the summer.

By the time Shaun hit high school, his career as an athlete had taken off. As a result, he had more on his mind than just his social life and grades—he was traveling to compete in fifteen or more snowboarding and skateboarding events every year. Luckily, Carlsbad High School was flexible, and "a really cool teacher," according to Shaun, helped him stay on track with his studies.

While many of Shaun's classmates were envious of the fact that he got to get out of school to travel to all of these events during the school year—not to mention to hobnob with celebrities like billionaire Richard Branson and rock star Slash (from Guns n' Roses)—they weren't jealous in the summertime, when they were all on break and Shaun had to catch up on all the homework he'd missed.

One of the most unique aspects of Shaun's life as a young adolescent was that he spent a lot of time around people who were older than he was. Because his friends ranged from fourteen to twenty-six years old, he found that some things that were funny to guys his own age weren't funny to people in their twenties. Shaun reports that, as an adolescent, he had to learn how to talk to older people.

In 2006, at the age of twenty, Shaun took his first Olympic gold medal at the Winter Games in the half-pipe, beating out fellow American Danny Kass with 46.8 points (out of a possible fifty) and establishing a new Olympic record for the category. This was a record that stood until Shaun returned to the Winter Olympics in 2010, when he improved it to 48.4 points in the men's half-pipe in his final run.

> Snowboarding was developed in the United States in the 1960s and '70s and became a Winter Olympics sport in 1998. Currently, skateboarding has not been accepted as an Olympic sport, but Shaun White would like to see that change.

At these Olympics, Shaun came to worldwide attention for his style on the slopes and his nickname, "The Flying Tomato." (In Italy, where he's very popular, that translates into *Il Pomodoro Volante*.) While Shaun initially embraced the title—and even tied his signature shoulder-length red hair back with a headband featuring his trademark tomato logo—*Rolling Stone Magazine* reports that he's grown tired of it. Shaun has since said he prefers another nickname: Animal, after the puppet character from *The Muppets*.

Tricks are an important part of both skateboarding and snowboarding competitions, and Shaun holds a number of records in this area. He's known as the first snowboarder ever to land back to back double corks at the Red Bull superpipe, as well as the only skater to land the frontside heelflip 540 body varial and the first skater to land a Cab 7 Melon Grab in vert skateboarding. His signature snowboard trick is the Double McTwist.

While Shaun has seen success in a variety of annual competitions in both snowboarding and skateboarding, the Winter X Games is where he has been dominant. Having competed every year since 2002—when he was just sixteen—Shaun has taken home ten gold medals, three silvers, and two bronzes. He is the first athlete ever to win back-to-back gold medals four years in a row at the Winter X Games SuperPipe.

Shaun is considered the most visible and well-known action sports athlete in the United States, and has raving fans all over the world. As a result, there are a lot of companies that would like to sponsor Shaun, but he's known for being selective as far as these commercial partnerships go. This has been important for him in maintaining his credibility to the snowboarding community—which cares a lot about authenticity and staying true to the sport—even as he has blown up into an international superstar.

Shaun has been sponsored by Volcom, Burton, Oakley, Sony PlayStation, Ubisoft, and Target. He has a line of video games, including Shaun White Skateboarding and Shaun White Snowboarding Road Trip. He has starred in a wide range of DVDs, including *Shaun White: Don't Look Down* from ESPN and *The Shaun White Album* (with an appearance by his old friend Tony Hawk).

> At Target, he created a line of clothing with his brother, called the White Collection.
> ⟿

Shaun told *Rolling Stone Magazine* that he plans to pursue both music and acting, but for now, he's at the height of his career and hopes to have ten or more years left competing in the two sports he's passionate about.

Right now, he's got his sights set on a third Winter Olympics in Sochi, Russia, in 2014—but he's also mentioned that if skateboarding were admitted to the Summer Olympics, he might take a year off from snowboarding just to focus on skating.

HOW WILL YOU ROCK THE WORLD?

I will rock the world by being a bike rider who does tricks. I will also be a snowboarder. I'm already practicing both. I like to snowboard with my friends, and last time we went, I did a kick flip off the ramp. If I become famous with my dirt bike racing or with snowboarding, I would tell everyone that I appreciate the encouragement my mom and dad have given me and also the help my brother has given me.

BRETT COX ☼ AGE 10

William Kamkwamba

1987– ⚬ INVENTOR AND ENGINEER ⚬ MALAWI (AFRICA)

This exquisite tale strips life down to its barest essentials, and once there finds reason for hopes and dreams.

—*PUBLISHERS WEEKLY* REVIEW OF *THE BOY WHO HARNESSED THE WIND: CREATING CURRENTS OF ELECTRICITY AND HOPE* BY WILLIAM KAMKWAMBA AND BRYAN MEALER

William had collected all the parts he needed and assembled them according to the diagram. The book said you could create electricity using a windmill, and that was exactly what William, age fourteen, intended to do. His family, like most families in Malawi, didn't have access to electricity, so he was determined. But no matter how much care and attention he'd taken in figuring out the words around the diagram—no matter how long it had taken him to find the parts he needed at the local junkyard—none of it would work if William couldn't get his hands on a bicycle dynamo.

What was worse, everyone thought he was crazy—even his mom! No one had ever seen the kind of windmill he was talking about, and if such a thing existed, they didn't believe he could build one using wood from local gum trees and items like an old, cast-off tractor fan and a bicycle frame.

William had dropped out of class that year, and the junkyard was right across from his old school. His former classmates had seen him digging through the trash and called out, "There's Kamkwamba, playing in the garbage again!" To him, all the pieces of old machinery, PVC tubes, and wires were a kind of treasure. To everyone else, they were junk. His mom worried that a boy who spent so much time digging through the garbage would never be able to find a wife.

William was walking down a road in the village with his cousin, Gilbert, when a bike sped past them. "Look!" said Gilbert. Attached to the back of this bike was the bicycle dynamo William had been looking for.

In a country like Malawi where bicycles are a common mode of transportation and electricity is scarce, these bicycle dynamos were a common sight—but they were still too expensive for the son of a poor farmer to purchase. Every time William saw one, he felt a little tortured.

But William's cousin Gilbert was the son of the local chief, and he had some pocket money on him. Gilbert ran up ahead to the bicyclist and offered him 500 kwacha (about $1.50 in US dollars) for that bicycle dynamo. It wasn't much, but the country was just coming through some tough economic times and jobs were still scarce, so the bicyclist didn't want to turn the money down. He took the cash from Gilbert, and Gilbert handed the bicycle dynamo to William.

By the time everything was in place, a large crowd had gathered. William could hear them as he stood high on the tower of the windmill he'd built; he recognized some of their faces as people who'd called him crazy. Reaching out, he grasped the two wires dangling from the heart of the machine and knotted their two ends together. He removed the piece of metal that kept the windmill's blades from turning, and then he clambered back down to the ground.

There he held a light bulb attached to one of the wires from the windmill. A breeze picked up, and the crowd hushed as the light bulb lit up—a flicker at first, but then a warm, steady glow.

"It's true!" said one person.

"Yes," said another, "the boy has done it."

Born in 1987 in Wimbe, Malawi, in Africa, William Kamkwamba is the eldest of seven siblings, and the only boy. Growing up, he got picked on by other boys at school because he didn't have an older brother to protect him, but he didn't let that get in the way of his studies. He did so well in junior high that he earned the right go on to high school—which is not free in Malawi, the way it is in the United States.

Unfortunately, when William was fourteen, his country was struck by a severe drought. This meant that his family no longer had the money it needed to send him to high school—in fact, they barely had enough to eat.

Like 80 percent of people in Malawi, William's family grew maize, or corn, which they prepared into a staple food called *nsima*. When the rains didn't come that year, his family's crops failed, producing just three bags of maize. In order to make those supplies last the whole year for the whole family, they ate only one meal a day, consisting of just three mouthfuls of nsima. Sometimes William's father went without his meal so there would be more food for the children.

> A bicycle dynamo is a small electrical generator that attaches to the wheel of a bicycle. Using basic electromagnetic principles, this generator transforms the motion of a moving bicycle tire into electricity, which is then used to power a headlamp on the front of the bike.

William decided to stay current on his classmates' schoolwork so that when his family had the money to send him to school again, he wouldn't be behind. This was when he turned to his school library, where he discovered *Using Energy*. This book showed diagrams explaining how windmills could be used to produce electricity and to pump water. The ability to pump water, for William, meant that he could bring irrigation to his family's farm, protecting them from future droughts. But first, William decided that he would learn how to produce electricity.

With the help of the school librarian, William figured out the parts he needed—and, in the process, taught himself not just his first words of English, but the basic principles of electromagnetics. William finished his first windmill in 2002, lighting up first one light bulb, then four, with homemade switches he made from PVC plastic. He even built a circuit breaker, using a magnet, modeled after an electric bell.

People came from miles around to see if the rumors they'd heard were true, and word began to spread about the boy who'd harnessed the wind. The *Daily Times* in Blantyre, the commercial capital of Malawi, wrote a story on Kamkwamba's windmill in November 2006, and the story was picked up by a blog site called Hacktivate. From there, it caught the attention of Emeka Okafor, program director for the TED Global Conference. Okafor invited William to fly to Arusha, Tanzania, for a TED Global event, during which audience members heard William's story and offered to help him fulfill his dreams of going back to school and building a second windmill for his family.

High school tuition in Malawi runs around $80 a year, in US dollars.

William went on to complete high school where he grew up and then to attend the African Leadership Academy in Johannesburg, South Africa. He built a bigger windmill, as he'd intended, to pump water for his family's farm, as well as a solar pump for a second, deeper well in his village that currently supplies water for six community taps.

William started a nonprofit organization called the Moving Windmills Project, which is dedicated to bringing community projects like the solar water pump system he created for his village to other villages in Malawi and beyond. He also wrote a book with American journalist Bryan Mealer called *The Boy Who Harnessed the Wind: Creating Currents of Electricity and Hope*, and is the subject of a documentary video.

In 2010, William became one of four recipients of the GO Ingenuity Award, a prize awarded by the Santa Monica-based nonprofit GO Campaign. With the grant, Kamkwamba will hold workshops for youth in his home village, teaching them how to make windmills and repair water pumps.

Currently, William attends Dartmouth College in New Hampshire for engineering.

HOW WILL YOU ROCK THE WORLD?

The way I would rock the world is in the field of engineering. The way that would have an effect on people is by my dream to help make transportation safer. I would install air bags for all passengers on trains, planes, and any other kind of transportation. Also I would add an automatic safety latch on the seat belts for school buses that get into severe crashes.

MARK GRASLE ⚛ AGE 14

Om Prakash Gurjar

1992– ✦ ACTIVIST ✦ INDIA

This is our right . . . [they] have to listen.
This is children's rights.
And if they are not abiding with that right,
we will work harder to make them hear.

—OM PRAKASH GURJAR

Walking the rows of the fields of the farm belonging to his family's landlord, Om was tired. Since the age of five, this was the only life he'd known; he worked all day, tending the fields in the hot sun—sometimes he even had to apply the chemicals that kept the bugs from eating the crops, chemicals that made his nose burn. Sometimes he had to take care of the animals in the landlord's barnyard, mucking out their stalls. It was hard work for a little boy, and Om knew that something was wrong.

He knew that not all children lived the way he did—some children got to go to school and learn how to read and write. Some children got to play soccer with other kids. Some kids weren't tired out from working every day.

As he bent to pull a weed that was poking up between the rows, Om remembered the group of people he'd met. They were people from outside his area, people who worked for an aid organization. They'd told him that what he was doing was something called child labor and that child labor was wrong. What if they were right? What if he was wasting his childhood here, working these endless hours for his family's landlord to pay off his family's debt?

The people from this aid organization wanted to help him. They wanted to free him from this work—but his family, Om knew, would be scared about not being able to pay off the debt they owed if they couldn't count on him to help. The landlord would also be upset—he would complain that he deserved Om's labor because Om's father owed him money. Where Om lived, no one thought there was anything wrong with sending a kid like him off to work.

But maybe, just maybe, the people from this aid organization could help Om make both his family and the landlord understand that he deserved something better than this—that he, as a kid, shouldn't be held responsible for something his father had done.

Om decided, then and there, that he would go back and talk with these people. Who knows? Maybe they'd be able to help him.

Om Prakash Gurjar was born in 1992 in Rajasthan, India. At the age of five, he was forced to join his family in indentured servitude to their landlord, in order to help pay back his father's debt. He was given two meals a day and beaten when he complained.

India introduced a new law in October 2006 banning children under the age of 14 from working as domestic servants or on food stalls. Even so, according to the TIMES OF INDIA, India is currently home to approximately 12.7 million child laborers, the largest number of any country—many of them in the ZARI, or gold thread, factories.

231

In 2000 Om met a group of activists from Bachpan Bachao Andolan (Save the Childhood Movement, or BBA), a nonprofit organization dedicated to ending child labor and child trafficking, and to rehabilitating exploited children. These activists worked to free Om—first by educating his parents about the rights of children, and second by exerting pressure on the landlord to free him.

Eventually these activists succeeded in their efforts, and Om went to live at Bal Ashram, BBA's home for kids like him, in Rajasthan. There he received education and training designed to help him create a better future for himself. He also came to understand that there are laws designed to protect children like him—laws such as UNICEF's Convention on the Rights of the Child, which apply not just in India, but all over the world.

At Bal Ashram, Om also got to experience something many of us take for granted in the United States: the chance to go to school. Om felt strongly about the importance of education, so before long, he volunteered to speak at a school about children's rights. Students and teachers alike were moved by his story as a former child slave, and Om was inspired to help create change.

His opportunity came when he realized that this school currently charged parents 100 rupees a year for each child's tuition. He knew from his education at Bal Ashram that public schools in Rajasthan were supposed to be free, so he contacted the local magistrate and demanded change.

A petition was put before the Jaipur Court, the high bench of the state of Rajasthan, and the court decided that the school was legally obliged to return all tuition money to the parents of its students—and that no tuition could be charged in the future. Om's case was cited by the Rajasthan State Human Rights Commission, and now public schools throughout Rajasthan are prohibited from charging tuition.

Working with the organization that rescued him, BBA, Om has helped approximately five hundred children from the Dausa and Alwar districts of Rajasthan to claim their rights and formally register with the government during birth registration campaigns. Since so many children exploited through child labor practices don't have any type of documentation proving how old they are or who their parents are, registering a birth certificate is an important first step to protecting children from forced labor.

Om also helped to establish a number of *Bal Mitra Grams*, or child-friendly villages, through BBA. These are villages that pledge to protect the rights of children by prohibiting child labor and reporting anyone engaged in such practices to the authorities.

> Unlike the United States, where every child is automatically issued a birth certificate, in India these certificates must be applied for.
> ⎯*ww*⎯

In recognition of his pioneering activism to end child labor and improve the lives of kids all over India, in 2006—at the age of fourteen—Om was awarded the International Children's Peace Prize, the world's highest honor for work benefiting children. The award was presented by former prime minister of South Africa F. W. de Klerk (who'd jointly received the Nobel Peace Prize with Nelson Mandela for helping to end apartheid) in Amsterdam, The Netherlands. A concert was held in Dam Square to honor Om and his message, featuring pop bands like UB40 and the Sugababes.

Om donated the €100,000 (about $140,250) prize money to two organizations: Stop Trafficking, Oppression and Prostitution of Children and Women in India and People's Welfare Service Committee in Nepal. Both organizations work to rescue children from child labor.

Upon his return from Amsterdam, Om was received by the president of India and several government cabinet ministers in order to discuss more effective measures against child labor in their country—and shortly after that, British Prime Minister Gordon Brown requested a meeting with Om during a visit to India. As part of this meeting, Brown announced that the government of the United Kingdom would invest €300 million in education for some of India's poorest children.

Om continues to work with BBA to rescue children from forced labor and to prevent the exploitation of children in India and beyond.

ROCK ON!

ALEC LOORZ

Alec Loorz is a young man with a plan. He founded Kids vs. Global Warming when he was twelve years old, and he was so effective in developing compelling presentations about the science of global warming that Al Gore invited him to train with the Climate Project to be an official presenter. At sixteen, he's given more than 250 presentations in the United States, and he spearheaded the iMatter March—an international event that included children from more than forty-three countries marching during Mother's Day week in May 2011 to tell the world that they care about global warming.

The Billy Elliot Boys

2008–2010 ◉ DANCERS ◉ UNITED STATES

We want to say to all the kids out there who
might want to dance, "Never give up."

—KIRIL KULISH, DURING HIS TONY AWARD ACCEPTANCE SPEECH
WITH TRENT KOWALIK AND DAVID ALVAREZ

After months of preparation, this was it: the audition of a lifetime. Kiril had seen the movie *Billy Elliot* and, like a lot of other people, he was crazy about it. The movie, written by Lee Hall, directed by Stephen Daldry, and choreographed by Peter Darling, told the story of a boy from a working class family in northern England who fell in love with dance while he was supposed to be getting boxing lessons at a local gym—and then went on to become a dancing sensation. This movie had been turned into a musical stage play in London, and now there were auditions for dancers to play the part of Billy in the US production. The destination? Broadway, New York.

Kiril took a deep breath and adjusted his dance shoes. He took a drink of water and prepared himself—these auditions, he'd been warned, could go on for hours. The judges would want to see him dancing not just ballet but whatever his favorite dance style was. They'd also want to know if he could sing and what key he was most comfortable in. If he was picked for the part, he'd be one of three boys who would take on the part of Billy, and they would alternate performances in order to keep up with the grueling New York production schedule.

Kiril sat in the green room with his family, waiting, thinking, hoping—and finally, the door opened. "Kiril Kulish?" the casting director asked.

"Right here," said Kiril, springing to his feet. He'd prepared, all these months, for this very moment—the chance to play Billy Elliot on Broadway. Did he have what it took?

BILLY ELLIOT: THE MUSICAL changed depending on which boy happened to be playing Billy. The choreography was different, as was some of the music—even the keys were changed, requiring adult actors to adjust their performances depending on which Billy was on stage.

Kiril Kulish—like Trent Kowalik and David Alvarez—was one of 1,500 boys nationwide who auditioned to dance the part of Billy Elliot when the production came to the United States in 2008. Like Trent and David, he was one of three boys picked to play the part, which would go on to win a total of ten Tony Awards for musical theater. Kiril got to share one of these awards with his two fellow Billys, recognizing their essential role in creating what the *New York Post* called "the best show you'll ever see!"

Lee Hall, who wrote the original screenplay for the movie, was amazed to discover that musical legend Elton John had seen the very first screening of the movie and wanted to make it into a musical play. They'd met in New York to talk about the project and agreed that in order for it to be a success, the original creative team from the movie would have to follow the story into the stage production. They'd worked out the songs and adapted the screenplay for the stage—but everything, Hall realized, rested on the boy who would wind up playing the all-important role of Billy.

What's more, they needed not one but three Billys, to make sure each dancer was fresh when it came time for him to go onstage. To Hall's amazement, they found those three Billy Elliot boys for the US production, and all three surpassed his hopes. What's more, he discovered that many of these kids were real-life Billy Elliots—boys who'd wanted to dance, against the odds, and who had wound up at the top of their field. He recognized their drive in the "sure, straightforward enjoyment of what they do" and noted that their pleasure in dance was simple, uncomplicated, and unpretentious. "To them, what they do is the most natural thing in the world," he said, "because they have found a way of expressing themselves."

Kiril's family originally hailed from Ukraine, but he was born in 1994 in San Diego, where he was raised. When he was just three years old, his sister introduced him to dance, and soon he was impressing audiences both in ballet—as the youngest member ever admitted to the Junior Company of the San Diego Ballet academy to win the Youth America Grand Prix competition—and ballroom dance. (He was the US National Champion in the junior division.) And if all that weren't enough, Kiril has also been hailed as a gifted concert pianist.

When Kiril was accepted to play Billy Elliot, he was thirteen years old. Now at sixteen, he's living in New York and Los Angeles, performing and working on creative projects.

Trent Kowalik was born in 1995, and like Kiril, he was thirteen when he took on the role of Billy Elliot. Unlike Kiril, he was a veteran of the Billy Elliot musical by the time he took the stage in New York—he'd played Billy in the original production in London.

Trent also started dance at just three years old, learning tap and ballet and, later, jazz and hip-hop in Long Island, New York, where he grew up. But at age four, Trent began instruction in Irish step dancing at the Inishfree School of Irish Dance, and by age six he was competing at the highest level of Irish dancing. By the time he auditioned to play Billy Elliot, Trent was a five-time undefeated North American Champion and a World Champion in Irish dance, not to mention the youngest American to ever win the World Championship.

Because of this, the eagle-eye talent scouts for *Billy Elliot: The Musical* had their eye on Trent from the moment they began looking for dancers who might play their lead role. Trent attended auditions in New York in November 2005 and again in November of 2006. In June of 2007, when the nationwide search narrowed down to fifteen boys, Trent was in that group; eventually, he made the final cut.

David Alvarez was born in Montreal, Canada, in 1994, the child of Cuban immigrants. Compared to his fellow Tony Award-winning Billys, he started dancing when he was practically an old man—eight years old! When David moved to San Diego, he had the chance to study at the San Diego Ballet, with (you guessed it) his future Billy costar, Kiril Kulish. David also studied with the California Ballet Company.

Unlike the Billy Elliot in the story, David's family has been behind his dance career the whole way. At age ten, when David was offered a full scholarship to the prestigious Jacqueline Kennedy Onassis School at the American Ballet Theater (ABT) in New York City, David's family left the West Coast and moved with him to the Big Apple so he could pursue his dream. At ABT, he was a featured performer in several productions— and now that he's done playing Billy Elliot, he's back there, continuing his ballet training. Like Kiril, David is also an accomplished classical pianist.

On June 7, 2009, Kiril Kulish, Trent Kowalik, and David Alvarez won a joint Tony Award for Best Actor in a Musical, the only performers to ever share a Tony Award for alternating performances in a single role. Since then, younger boys have gone on to play Billy Elliot, creating new opportunities for young dancers to step into the spotlight on Broadway and across America.

HOW WILL YOU ROCK THE WORLD?

My favorite way to rock the world would be to become a professional dancer. Studying dancing teaches you to stay focused and develop self-discipline. I'd like to be someone like Mikhail Baryshnikov or Rudolf Nureyev. I'd also like to educate people about dancing, ballet in particular. Some people think that ballet is easy or that it's only for girls. All dancers are athletes, but most people don't realize that.

LUCAS THREEFOOT ☼ AGE 12

Recommended Resources

We have listed below the resources used to research the amazing boys profiled in this book and have also included some additional materials that you can check out if you want to know more about these heroes.

BOOKS

Adair, Gene. *Thomas Alva Edison: Inventing the Electric Age*. New York: Oxford University Press, 1996.

Agins, Teri. *The End of Fashion: How Marketing Changed the Clothing Business Forever*. New York: HarperCollins, 2000.

Aldred, Cyril. *Tutankhamun's Egypt*. New York: Charles Scribner's Sons, 1972.

Baldwin, Neil. *Edison: Inventing the Century*. New York: Hyperion, 1995.

Barry, James. *The Berlin Olympics: 1936 Black American Athletes Counter Nazi Propaganda*. New York: Franklin Watts, 1975.

Beahm, George. *Stephen King: America's Best Loved Boogeyman*. Kansas City: Andrews McMeel Publishing, 1999.

Beahm, George. *Stephen King Country: The Illustrated Guide to the Sites and Sights That Inspired the Modern Master of Horror*. Philadelphia: Running Press, 1999.

Boardingham, Robert. *The Young Picasso*. New York: Universe Publishing, 1997.

Brier, Bob. *The Murder of Tutankhamen*. New York: G.P. Putman's Sons, 1998.

Brindell Fradin, Dennis. *Remarkable Children: Twenty Who Made History*. Boston: Little, Brown and Company, 1987.

Burch, Joann J. *Chico Mendes: Defender of the Rain Forest*. Brookfield, CT: Millbrook Press, 1994.

Chernev, Irving. *Twelve Great Chess Players and Their Best Games*. Mineola, NY: Courier Dover Publications, 1995.

Cobb, Vicki. *Truth on Trial: The Story of Galileo Galilei*. New York: Coward, McCann & Geoghegan, 1979.

Davis, Wade. *The Wayfinders: Why Ancient Wisdom Matters in the Modern World*. Toronto, ON: House of Anansi Press Inc., 2009.

Feinstein, Barry, Daniel Kramer, and Jim Marshall. *Early Dylan*. Boston: Bullfinch Press, 1999.

Ford, Barbara. *Howard Carter: Searching for King Tut*. New York: W. H. Freeman and Company, 1995.

Freedman, Russell. *The Life and Death of Crazy Horse*. New York: Holiday House, 1996.

Galilei, Galileo. *Discoveries and Opinions of Galileo*. Translated by Stillman Drake. New York: Random House, 1957.

Freedman, Russell. *Out of Darkness: The Story of Louis Braille*. New York: Clarion Books, 1997.

Green, Robert. *Tutankhamun*. New York: Franklin Watts, 1996.

Guttmacher, Peter. *Crazy Horse*. New York: Chelsea House Publishers, 1994.

Hardorff, Richard G. *The Surrender and Death of Crazy Horse: A Source Book about the Tragic Episode in Lakota History*. Spokane, WA: The Arthur H. Clark Company, 1998.

Henson, Matthew. *Matthew A. Henson's Historic Arctic Journey: The Classic Account of One of the World's Greatest Black Explorers*. Guilford, CT: Globe Pequot, 2009.

Hillsborough, Romulus. *Shinsengumi: The Shogun's Last Samurai Corps*. Tokyo: Tuttle Publishing, 2005.

Hoffman, Phyllis Norton. *Honey, It's All in the Shoes: Celebrating the Footsteps of the Contemporary Woman*. Deerfield Beach, FL: HCI Books, 2009.

Hoffmann, Frank W. and William G. Bailey. *Fashion & Merchandising Fads*. London: Psychology Press, 1994.

Hoving, Thomas. *Tutankhamun: The Untold Story*. New York: Simon and Schuster, 1978.

Hughes, Libby. *Nelson Mandela: Voice of Freedom*. New York: Dillon Press, 1992.

Humphries, Patrick. *Absolutely Dylan*. New York: Viking Studio, 1991.

Ireland, Karin. *Albert Einstein*. Englewood Cliffs, NJ: Silver Burdett Press, 1989.

Josephson, Judith Pinkerton. *Jesse Owens: Track and Field Legend*. Springfield, NJ: Enslow Publishers, 1997.

Kamkwamba, William, and Bryan Mealer. *The Boy Who Harnessed the Wind*. New York: William Morrow, 2009.

Kerst, Friedrich. *Mozart: The Man and the Artist Revealed in His Own Words*. Translated by Henry Krehbiel. New York: Dover Publications, 1965.

King, Stephen. *On Writing*. New York: Scribner, 2000.

Koenig, Viviane. *The Ancient Egyptians: Life in the Nile Valley*. Brookfield, CT: The Millbrook Press, 1992.

Komroff, Manuel. *Mozart*. New York: Alfred A. Knopf, 1956.

Lee, Bruce. *Striking Thoughts: Bruce Lee's Wisdom for Everyday Living*. Boston: Turtle Publishing, 2000.

Lee, Bruce. *Words from a Master*. Chicago: Contemporary Books, 1999.

Lee, Stan, and George Mair. *Excelsior! The Amazing Life of Stan Lee*. New York: Simon and Schuster, 2002.

Lesinski, Jeanne. *Bill Gates*. Minneapolis: Lerner Publications Company, 2000.

MacLachlan, James. *Galileo Galilei*. New York: Oxford University Press, 1997.

Mailer, Norman. *Portrait of Picasso as a Young Man*. New York: Atlantic Monthly Press, 1995.

Mandela, Nelson. *Mandela: An Illustrated Autobiography*. Boston: Little, Brown & Co., 1994.

McNeill, Sarah. *Ancient Egyptian People*. Brookfield, CT: The Millbrook Press, 1996.

McPherson, Stephanie. *Ordinary Genius: The Story of Albert Einstein*. Minneapolis: Carolrhoda Books, Inc., 1995.

Millard, Anne. *The World of the Pharaoh*. New York: Peter Bedrick Books, 1998.

Mitchell, Barbara. *The Wizard of Sound: A Story about Thomas Edison*. Minneapolis: Carolrhoda Books, 1997.

Muhlberger, Richard. *What Makes a Picasso a Picasso?* New York: Viking, 1994.

Murdoch, David. *Tutankhamun: The Life and Death of the Pharaoh*. New York: DK Publishing, 1998.

Nuwer, Hank. *The Legend of Jesse Owens*. New York: Franklin Watts, 1998.

Owens, Jesse. *Blackthink: My Life as Black Man and White Man*. New York: William Morrow, 1970.

Parker, Steve. *Thomas Edison and Electricity*. New York: Harper Collins, 1992.

Pelé and Robert L. Fish. *My Life and the Beautiful Game: The Autobiography of Soccer's Biggest Star*. New York: Doubleday, 1977.

Rees, Rosemary. *The Ancient Egyptians*. Crystal Lake, IL: Heinemann Library, 1997.

Reinfeld, Fred. *The Immortal Games of Capablanca*. Mineola, NY: Courier Dover Publications, 1990.

Reino, Joseph. *Stephen King: The First Decade, Carrie to Pet Sematary*. Boston: Twayne Publishers, 1988.

Revkin, Andrew. *The Burning Season: The Murder of Chico Mendes and the Fight for the Amazon Rain Forest.* Boston: Houghton Mifflin, 1990.

Ribowsky, Mark. *Signed, Sealed, and Delivered: The Soulful Journey of Stevie Wonder.* New York: John Wiley and Sons, 2010.

Richmond, Ray, and Antonia Coffman, eds. *The Simpsons: A Complete Guide to our Favorite Family.* New York: HarperCollins, 1997.

Roberts, Russell. *The Rulers of Ancient Egypt.* San Diego, CA: Lucent Books, 1999.

Ross, Betty. *Mexico: Land of Eagle and Serpent.* New York: Taylor & Francis, 1965.

Saidman, Anne. *Stephen King: Master of Horror.* Minneapolis: Lerner Publications Company, 1992.

Sample, Tim, and Steve Bither. "Chester Greenwood" in *Maine Curiosities*, 3rd ed. Guilford, CT: Globe Pequot, 2011.

Sassoon, Vidal. *Vidal: The Autobiography.* London: Pan Macmillan, 2010.

Schoch, Robert M., and Robert Aquinas McNally. *Voyages of the Pyramid Builders.* New York: Penguin, 2004.

Severance, John B. *Einstein: Visionary Scientist.* New York: Clarion Books, 1999.

Shoumatoff, Alex. *The World is Burning: Murder in the Rain Forest.* Boston: Little, Brown and Company, 1990.

Spitz, Bob. *Dylan: A Biography.* New York: McGraw-Hill, 1989.

St. George, Judith. *Crazy Horse.* New York: G.P. Putman's Sons, 1994.

Wallace, James, and Jim Erickson. *Hard Drive: Bill Gates and the Making of the Microsoft Empire.* New York: John Wiley & Sons, Inc., 1992.

Weatherly, Myra. *Yo-Yo Ma: Internationally Acclaimed Cellist.* Mankato, MN: Compass Point Books, 2007.

White, Michael, and John Gibbin. *Einstein: A Life in Science.* New York: Dutton Publishing, 1993.

White, Michael. *Galileo Galilei: Inventor, Astronomer and Rebel.* Woodbridge, CT: Blackbirch Press, 1999.

Williams, Tenley and James S. Brady. *Stevie Wonder.* New York: Infobase Publishing, 2001.

Wukovits, John F. *Stephen King.* San Diego, CA: Lucas Books, 1999.

Young, Percy. *Mozart.* New York: The Bookwright Press, 1988.

ARTICLES

BBC News. "Indian Boy Wins World Peace Prize." (November 19, 2006). http://news.bbc.co.uk/2/hi/south_asia/6164134.stm.

Brendle, Anna. "Profile: African-American North Pole Explorer Matthew Henson." *National Geographic News* (January 15, 2003). http://news.nationalgeographic.com/news/2003/01/0110_030113_henson.html.

Brown, Emma. "Mau Piailug, Micronesian Who Sailed by Navigating Sun and Stars, Dies at 78." *Washington Post* (July 21, 2010). http://www.washingtonpost.com/wp-dyn/content/article/2010/07/20/AR2010072002941.html.

Clayton, Jeremy. "Talking with . . . Taboo." *Giant Life* (July 1, 2009). giantmag.com/the-magazine/giant-magazine-staff/talking-withtaboo/.

Cocks, Jay. "The Folk Musician." *Time* (June 8, 1998). http://www.time.com/time/magazine/article/0,9171,988504,00.html.

Coyle, Chris. "The Shaun White Interview." *Transworld Snowboarding* (October 7, 2003). http://snowboarding.transworld.net/1000026824/uncategorized/the-shaun-white-interview/.

Detourn, Nico. "Microsoft's Fiscal Millennium." *The Motley Fool* (July 28, 2000). http://www.fool.com/news/2000/msft000728.htm.

Grant, Meg. "Will Smith Interview: Will Power." *Reader's Digest* (December 2006). http://www.rd.com/family/will-smith-interview/4/.

Green, Jesse. "The Peter Pans of Broadway." *New York Theater* (October 26, 2008). http://nymag.com/arts/theater/features/51543/.

Jaggi, Maya. "All Rage and Heart." *The Guardian* (May 2, 2008). www.guardian.co.uk/books/2008/may/03/featuresreviews .guardianreview13.

Keegan, Rebecca Winters. "The Legend of Will Smith." *Time* (November 29, 2007). http://www.time.com/time/magazine/ article/0,9171,1689234-1,00.html.

Keller, Helen. "Braille, the Magic Wand of the Blind." American Foundation for the Blind (n.d.). http://www.afb.org/Section.asp?Secti onID=86&DocumentID=1187.

Kuniansky, Neal. "eBraille: Making Braille Easy Around the World." Paper given at 66th IFLA Council and General Conference, Jerusalem, Israel, August 13, 2000.

Long, Tony. "December 4, 1858: It Was Very Cold the Day Chester Greenwood Was Born." *Wired* (December 4, 2007). http://www .wired.com/science/discoveries/news/2007/12/dayintech_1204.

O'Connor, J. J., and E. F. Robertson. "Blaise Pascal." School of Mathematics and Statistics, University of St. Andrews (December 1996). http://www-history.mcs.st-andrews.ac.uk/history/Biographies/ Pascal.html.

Phillips, Sarah. "A Brief History of Facebook." *The Guardian* (July 24, 2007). http://www.guardian.co.uk/technology/2007/jul/25/media .newmedia.

Robertson, Campbell. "The Boys of 'Billy' Get Ready to Lead." *The New York Times* (April 22, 2008). http://www.nytimes.com/2008/04/22/ theater/22bill.html.

Smith, Sean. "The $4 Billion Man." *Newsweek* (April 15, 2007). http:// www.newsweek.com/2007/04/15/the-4-billion-man.html.

Smith, Sean. "The 50 Smartest People in Hollywood." *Entertainment Weekly* (November 28, 2007). http://insidemovies.ew.com/2007/11/ 28/smart-list-intr/.

Time. "The Time 100" (May 2, 2011).

Vargas, Jose Antonio. "The Face of Facebook." *The New Yorker* (September 20, 2010). http://www.newyorker.com/ reporting/2010/09/20/100920fa_fact_vargas?currentPage=all.

White, Dana. "will.i.am's Aha! Moment." *O Magazine* (May 2009). http://www.oprah.com/spirit/Black-Eyed-Peas-Singer-williams-Aha-Moment.

WEBSITES

About the White House. "The Presidents." http://www.whitehouse.gov/ about/presidents/.

Bachpan Bachoa Andolan: Save the Childhood Movement. bba.org.in/.

Billy Elliot: The Musical. billyelliotbroadway.com.

Bio.com. biography.com.

The Black Eyed Peas. blackeyedpeas.com/.

The Comic Book Database. "Stan Lee—'Stanley Martin Lieber'." http:// comicbookdb.com/creator.php?ID=98.

Cultural China. "Emperor Kangxi: The Emperor Who Reigned for the Longest Period in Chinese History." http://history.cultural-china .com/en/46History211.html.

Elvis Presley. elvis.com.

Encyclopedia of World Biography. notablebiographies.com/.

Faces of America. "Yo-Yo Ma." www.pbs.org/wnet/facesofamerica/profiles/ yo-yo-ma/7/.

History of China. "Emperor Kangxi." http://www.history-of-china.com/ qing-dynasty/kangxi-emperor.htm.

International Children's Peace Prize. "2006 Om Prakash Gurjar." http:// childrenspeaceprize.org/childrens-peace-price/price2006/.

Mirick, John. "William H. Gates III: Before Microsoft." http:// ei.cs.vt.edu/~history/Gates.Mirick.html.

Museo Salvatore Ferragamo. http://www.museoferragamo.it/en/scopri.php.

National Park Service. "John Quincy Adams Biography." http://www
.nps.gov/adam/jqabio.htm.

Public Broadcasting Service. "The Long Walk of Nelson Mandela."
http://www.pbs.org/wgbh/pages/frontline/shows/mandela/.

Public Broadcasting Service. "U.S.–Mexican War." http://www.pbs.org/
kera/usmexicanwar/war/.

Shaun White. shaunwhite.com.

The Times of India. "Hrithik Roshan: Profile." http://timesofindia
.indiatimes.com/topic/Hrithik-Roshan.

William Kamkwamba. http://williamkamkwamba.typepad.com/
williamkamkwamba/.

Yo-Yo Ma. http://www.yo-yoma.com/yo-yo-ma-biography.

MOVIES

Amadeus, 1984, Milos Forman

Compassion in Exile: The Life of the 14th Dalai Lama, 1993, Mickey Lemle

The Curse of King Tut's Tomb, 2006, Russel Mulcahy

Dragon: The Bruce Lee Story, 1993, Rob Cohen

Elvis, 2005, James Steven Sadwith

Invictus, 2009, Clint Eastwood

No Direction Home: Bob Dylan, 2005, Martin Scorsese

Okita Soji, 1974, Masanobu Deme

Smoke Signals, 1998, Chris Eyre

The Social Network, 2010, David Fincher

Vidal Sassoon: The Movie, 2010, Craig Teper

Wayfinders, 1998, Gail K. Evenari

Endnotes

1. The ages of the individuals who gave quotes for the "How Will You Rock" sections of this book reflect the age of the person at the time the quote was given.

2. Galileo Galilei, *Discoveries and Opinions of Galileo*, trans. Stillman Drake (New York: Random House, 1957), 237–238.

3. The information presented in all Rock On spotlights was gathered from public sources.

4. Friedrich Kerst, *Mozart: The Man and the Artist Revealed in His Own Words*, trans. Henry Krehbiel (New York: Dover Publications, 1965), 6.

5. Irving Chernev, *Twelve Great Chess Players and Their Best Games* (Mineola, NY: Courier Dover Publications, 1995), 181.

6. Jesse Owens, *Blacjthink: My Life as a Black Man and White Man* (New York: William Morrow, 1970), 163.

7. Nelson Mandela, Mandela: An Illustrated Autobiography (New York: Little, Brown, 1996), 52.

8. Nelson Mandela, "Nelson Mandela's Statement from the Dock at the Opening of the Defence Case in the Rivonia Trial," *Nelson Mandela International Day*, http://www.un.org/en/events/mandeladay/court _statement_1964.shtml.

9. His Holiness the Dalai Lama, "A Clean Environments Is a Human Right," *His Holiness the 14th Dalai Lama of Tibet*. Accessed May 23, 2012. http://dalailama.com/messages/environment/clean -environment.

10. Myra Weatherly, *Yo-Yo Ma: Internationally Acclaimed Cellist* (Mankato, MN: Compass Point Books, 2007), 22.

11. Weatherly, 23.

12. "Letter from Bill and Melinda Gates," *Bill and Melinda Gates Foundation*. Accessed November 11, 2011. http://www.gates foundation.org/about/Pages/bill-melinda-gates-letter.aspx.

13. Maya Jaggi, "All Rage and Heart," *The Guardian*, May 3, 2008. http://www.guardian.co.uk/books/2008/may/03/featuresreviews .guardianreview13.

14. Robert Capriccioso, "Sherman Alexie: American Indian Filmmaker/ Writer Talks with Robert Capriccioso," *Identity Theory*, March 23, 2003. http://www.identitytheory.com/interviews/alexie_interview.html.

15. "A Perfect Professional Has Come to Stay," *The Hindu*, 8 August 2000. http://www.hinduonnet.com/2000/08/18/stories/09180221.htm.

16. "Facebook trades below expectations," *NBC Nightly News with Brian Williams* video segment, May 18, 2012. http://www.msnbc.msn.com /id/3032619/ns/NBCNightlyNews/#47482551.

17. "Mark Zuckerberg," *Forbes*, March 2012. http://www.forbes.com /profile/mark-zuckerberg/.